AF587393

Chronicles of the Road: Five Nations, Five Artists
By Barnabas Ticha Muvhuti

Chronicles of the Road: Five Nations, Five Artists

Barnabas Ticha Muvhuti

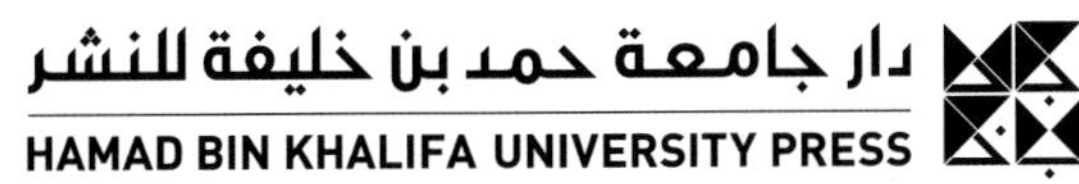

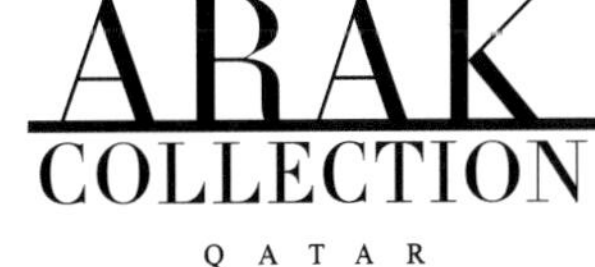

Hamad Bin Khalifa University Press
P.O. Box 5825
Doha, Qatar

www.hbkupress.com

First English edition in 2024

ISBN: 9789927170645

Printed in Doha-Qatar

Qatar National Library Cataloging-in-Publication (CIP)

Muvhuti, Barnabas Ticha, author.

Chronicles of the road : five nations, five artists / Barnabas Ticha Muvhuti. - First English edition. Doha, Qatar : Hamad Bin Khalifa University Press, 2024.

112 pages : color illustrations ; 30 cm. - (ARAK Collection Qatar)

Includes bibliographical references (pages 109-110).

ISBN 978-992-717-064-5

1. Art, Southern African -- 21st century -- History and criticism. 2. Artists -- Africa, Southern -- Biography. 3. Seibeb, Rudolf, 1964- 4. Artists -- Namibia -- Biography. 5. Phetogo, Thebe, 1993- 6. Artists -- Botswana -- Biography. 7. Chishimba, Mutale Kalinosi, 1971- 8. Artists -- Zambia -- Biography. 9. Guambe, Nelly, 1987- 10. Artists -- Mozambique -- Biography. 11. Luzamba, Lutanda Zemba, 1973- 12. Artists -- Congo (Democratic Republic) -- Biography. I. Title.

N7391.7 .M89 2024
709.68– dc 23

202429019199

TABLE OF CONTENTS

ACKNOWLEDGEMENTS

I am indebted to the ARAK Team for funding my research trip to the selected Southern African countries, as well as the five artists included in this project—Rudolf Seibeb, Thebe Phetogo, Nelly Guambe, (Victor) Mutale Kalinosi Chishimba, and Lutanda Zemba Luzamba—for welcoming me into their studios and spaces for interviews.

I would like to thank Dr. Andrew Mulenga, a Zambian Art Historian and the deputy vice chancellor at Open Window University for Creative Arts, for providing the introductory essay, and Fadzai Veronica Muchemwa, the deputy director and curator for Contemporary Art of the National Gallery of Zimbabwe, for editing the essays in the project.

In Namibia, I would like to thank Frieda Luhl of the Project Room for linking me up with Rudolf Seibeb, Ndeenda Shivute-Nakapunda, the chief curator of the National Art Gallery of Namibia, and the curator and artist, Jo Rogge, for insights on Seibeb, as well as Ricardo Stramiss, the artist's assistant, who also interpreted my interview with the artist.

In Botswana, I would like to thank Tumelo Lekolwane for accompanying me to Matsieng Footprints and for helping engage the custodian of the site.I am indebted to Andrew Mulenga and artist Stary Mwaba for showing me some of the cultural spaces in Lusaka. With the language barrier, I am not sure if I would have managed finding my way in Maputo without the assistance of artist Nelsa Guambe and Falcao. Nelsa, who is Nelly's sister, also took me to her atelier and to the Nucleo de Arte, an important institution in the development of modern art in Mozambique.

I would also like to thank Dr. Ashraf Jamal from South Africa and Jamil Parasol Osmar from Angola for the enriching conversations we had in Doha.

THE RESEARCH PROCESS

This project is the culmination of my six-month writing fellowship with the ARAK Collection. I worked on it from May to October 2023. With my experiences embedded in it, the project adopts an informal and subjective style of writing aimed at making it accessible to a broad audience.

When the works in the ARAK Collection were unveiled to me, I opted to research on a quintet of artists from five different countries in the Southern African Development Community (SADC). They are Botswana's Thebe Phetogo (b. 1993), the Democratic Republic of Congo's Lutanda Zemba Luzamba (b. 1973), Namibia's Rudolf Seibeb (b. 1964), Mozambique's Nelly Guambe (b. 1987), and Zambia's (Victor) Mutale Kalinosi Chishimba (b. 1971). I deliberately skirted over the many South African artists in the collection because most of the writings on art from the SADC region focus on the country. This is due to its high concentration of art institutions in the form of galleries, museums, and universities, art historians and critics, as well as publishing platforms. Thus, South Africa leads the charge when it comes to activity and writings on art history and the contemporary arts scene. Therefore, this project aims to expand the canon by directing the reader towards artists from nations neighbouring South Africa.

On the 19th of July, I left Cape Town on a road trip that took me to Windhoek past the Noordoewer/Vioolsdrif border crossing, proceeding to Gaborone via Buitepos border post, then to Lusaka past the multinational Kazungula Bridge. From Zambia's capital city, I headed to Chimoio past the Forbes border post, after some brief stopovers in Livingstone, Victoria Falls, Bulawayo, and Mutare.From Chimoio, I then proceeded to Maputo before returning to South Africa past the Lebombo border on the 11th of August. This was my fieldwork research trip during which I met and engaged with the selected artists and cultural practitioners in the art sector.

My interviews with them were semi-structured, allowing me to draw as much information as possible from them. The main motivation for the trip was to gain an in-depth understanding of parts of the Southern African region, or the selected artists' respective contexts which inform their practices. In the process, I also engaged strangers on the buses, the taxis, and on the streets. At times, I also diverted to outlying areas like Okahandja, where I met Seibeb, Matsieng, the heritage site referenced by Phetogo and Ndeke Village, where Mutale resides and works from.

I realised that immigration officials were only allowing me a maximum of ten days, of which I required less. At the Mozambican border, I was asked to produce a COVID-19 vaccination certificate, which was quite unusual. I did not have to travel to the Democratic Republic of Congo as Luzamba is based in Cape Town. Where necessary, I did follow-up engagements with the artists via WhatsApp. In the process, one thing led to another and ideas and theories developed as the interactions ensued. I then travelled to Doha, Qatar in November to take a closer look at the artworks of the selected artists, and to have a cultural experience of the city and country where the collection is housed.

The research employs a biographical approach. Oral historian Joanna Bornat indicates that "biographical methods is an umbrella term for an assembly of loosely related, variously titled activities [which include]: narrative, life history, oral history, autobiography, biographical interpretive methods, storytelling, auto/biography, reminiscence" (2008: 344).[1] This project is quite experimental in that it brings together three artists who do figurative work and two who are into abstraction. It is an attempt to find common ground in their diverse practices through an exploration of their respective local contexts.

[1]Bornat, Janna. 2008 . 'Biographical methods'. In: Alasuutari, Pertti; Bickman, Leonard and Brannen, Julia eds. The Sage Handbook of Social Research Methods. London, UK: Sage, pp. 344_356 .

INTRODUCTION

By Andrew Mulenga

Botswana, Democratic Republic of Congo (DRC), Mozambique, Namibia, and Zambia. That is a line-up that almost reads like the Frontline States, or at least an iteration of them, one that would later morph into another collective of Southern African states, the Southern African Development Community (SADC).[2]

In 1970, the Frontline States were established to coordinate their responses to apartheid and develop a common stance against both the liberation movement and the apartheid regime. The creation of the Frontline States provided a fresh front in the struggle against apartheid, which was much-needed for the liberation movement in South Africa.

The Southern African countries, Angola, Botswana, Lesotho, Mozambique, Swaziland, Tanzania, Zambia, and, starting in 1980, Zimbabwe, provided regional support for the end of apartheid and the beginning of democracy in South Africa. Indeed, not exactly the list of countries earlier mentioned but one that had foreshadowed the SADC to which now even South Africa belongs. Notwithstanding, South Africa is the most powerful nation in the region both economically and, perhaps, culturally, allowing it to have an external impact on the creative industries through outputs such as dance, music, film, and visual arts. Dominance by South Africa is not a recent development. Since most of the SADC member states were heavily dependent on South Africa, it was difficult for Southern African nations to put sanctions on and isolate the country, even during the Frontline States' era.

South Africa was—and still is—a major economic factor; a lot of Frontline States' citizens were employed in South Africa, particularly in the mines. They also had direct connections to the government of South Africa; one example is Botswana, which borders South Africa. Sir Seretse Khama, the president of Botswana, freely acknowledged that, despite his affiliation with the Frontline States, he also needed to maintain cordial relations with South Africa.

Furthermore, these nations' combined efforts fell short of South Africa's military power, which was repeatedly employed to force these nations to surrender to its will. This is where the intricate political and geographic history of Southern Africa, or more accurately, geopolitical histories, come together.

Nevertheless, it may be claimed that, in terms of national art histories, the SADC countries included in the ARAK Collection are notably underappreciated and underrepresented in the global capitals, where some forms of representations of modern and contemporary African art exist. It is possible to argue that the nations represented by the artists in this collection have thus been hidden from examination within a more comprehensive comparative context.

[2]Frontline States, South African History Online (https://www.sahistory.org.za/article/frontline-states).

The ARAK Collection therefore provides a remarkable case study for divergent trajectories of the compendium of modern and contemporary African art. Indeed, it appears from the outside that only South African artists are valued and considered significant enough to have international appeal, as seen by the inclusion of their artwork in esteemed collections located outside Africa, as well as by the renowned Zeitz MOCAA, situated in the heart of Cape Town in South Africa. This is partially due to the delayed development of an academic and commercial art scene in most SADC nations outside of South Africa. This is worsened by the absence of other facilities for art production and display, such as galleries and fairs, as well as a lack of political will to provide policy frameworks for local and international distribution of creative outputs.

The knowledge of modern and contemporary art from the SADC region outside South Africa, including its documentation, theorisation, and chronicling, remains severely lacking. Yet it can contribute to the rich and vibrant discourses of postcolonial, decolonial, transnational, and global art.

The only way interest of collectors, galleries, and `museums from around the world is if they are regularly featured and discussed in significant publications such as, *African Artists From 1882 to Now*, edited by an eminent United States-based, Nigerian scholar, Chika Okeke-Agulu.

As Okeke-Agulu points out, the book examines African artists and modern and contemporary art spanning more than a century. Its scope and ambition are unprecedented, and it was certain to spark lively discussions about "African modernity, but also the place of the continent its people and cultural production during the age of colonization and beyond."[3] Even in such a publication of a broad scope, Okeke-Agulu points out that the book, African Artists From 1882 to Now, emphatically showcases just a handful of African artists who have received international attention in recent years and that they are "but a small part of a broader and deeper underacknowledged field of impressive and profound artistic production."[4]

Nevertheless, because he too is a voice from outside the West, North, and South African art power circles, it is crucial that art historians, such as Barnabas Ticha Muvhuti, who has written the several essays commissioned by the ARAK Collection, are given the responsibility of assisting in the reasonably obscured artists' elevation through a series of essays that are the result of embedded research, a task granted to him by the ARAK Collection, thus making a scholar from the region in charge of knowledge production, Africans writing African stories, as it were.

[3] Chika Okeke-Agulu. 2021. Introduction, African Artists: From 1882 to Now by Phaidon, Underwood, J.L. Okeke-Agulu, C. (eds.).

[4] Ibid.

The ARAK Collection defies the obscuring and ignoring of art from the SADC region, even though it is easy to point fingers at this statement for reductionism or unwarranted over- simplifications regarding why the countries it features are frequently left out of the mainstream modern and contemporary African art market. Additionally, the painters from the SADC region included here have their artwork shown prominently in the collection kept in Doha, Qatar. Abbreviated as "ARAK" after the collector AbdulRahman Al Khulaifi, ARAK is the most comprehensive collection of Sub-Saharan African art in the Gulf. Almost 3000 artworks created by over 250 artists from around the world are presently housed in the collection.

In addition to being an exploration of the interco- nnectedness and complexity of these regions' cultures, Muvhuti's travels to Botswana, Mozambique, Namibia, and Zambia for his preliminary research were also an adventure of discovery. He found that the region's figurative and abstract art had a lot in common after looking closely at the select artists' works. These observations in turn made him question from an analytical standpoint whether these figurative and abstract works should be separated.

Observing Namibian painter Rudolf Seibeb at work in his studio at the Okahandja Craft Market, where he selects discovered objects to include into his paintings, was one of Muvhuti's[5] most unforgettable experiences. Muvhuti describes the artist as a visual storyteller observing that viewers have likened his work to that of Jean-Michel Basquiat because it is driven by a fearless creativity and yet engages in topical local matters like the Fishrot scandal. The Icelandic fishing corporation, Samherji, paid millions of euros to bribe high level officials in Namibia for trawling rights, using tax havens, including Cyprus and the Marshall Islands, according to the Fishrot allegations made public by whistleblower Johannes Stefansson.[6]

Meeting with Thebe Phetogo was yet another pivotal moment for Muvhuti. As an artist, Phetogo contests the mainstream narrative of three chiefs who negotiated for British protection as the basis of Botswana's unity and peacefulness, much like what had happened to the Lozi people in present day Zambia. The narrative has a white hand to it. Phetogo would like the Batswana people to revisit myths associated with precolonial Botswana, such as the story of Matsieng, the site which appears in his paintings. Matsieng is a heritage site and a location shrouded in consecrated mythology. Phetogo reimagines these myths and dispels writings that may otherwise cast it in doubt as a place that is considered by the people of Botswana to be the cradle of humanity.

[5]Barnabas T. Muvhuti, personal communication during field trip, Lusaka, Zambia, 2023.

[6]THE FISHROT SCANDAL, Platform to Protect Whistleblowers in Africa. https://www.pplaaf.org/cases/fishrot.html#, (accessed on 25/12/23).

It was symbolic for him to meet (Victor) Mutale Kalinosi Chishimba at his studio on the outskirts of Lusaka, given his present position in Zambian art circles, his preference for working more alone, and the fact that apprentices approach him rather than the other way around. Like Phetogo, Mutale is equally inspired by the past, and despite him not being from Botswana from where the San peoples hail, some of his work is inspired by the San. Though inspired by the San, they are in fact his own invention and he calls them his 'Kalidrawings'—his own form of drawings. In doing so, he is in the company of others like El Loko (Togo) whose 'Cosmic Alphabet' is a permanent feature of the sixth floor at the Zeitz MOCAA. Muvhuti observes that nations in Southern Africa have not recognised the role of the San as the first peoples of the region. In nations where their descendants still dwell, none of them have recognised their language as official; therefore, Kalinosi's work draws our attention to this neglected heritage.

Among the artists in the collection, perhaps Lutanda Zemba Luzamba is the artist who embodies notions of the national' artist in the SADC region more than anyone else. Hailing from the Democratic Republic of Congo, he studied in Zambia at the Evelyn Hone College but has made base in Cape Town. He primarily depicts the La Sape tradition, which is centered on the cities of Kinshasa in the Democratic Republic of the Congo and Brazzaville in the Republic of the Congo. The name 'La Sape' is an acronym for 'Société des Ambianceurs et des Personnes Élégantes' (French for 'Society of Ambiance-Makers and Elegant People') and alludes to the French slang word 'sape,' which means 'clothes' or 'sapé,' which means 'dressed up.' The western-inspired tradition consists primarily of men dressing up in the latest styles of suits and hats, wearing expensive French labels like Givenchy, Balmain, Christian Dior, Pierre Cardin, and Louis Vuitton, often in sharp contrast to their dingy living quarters.

But in the ARAK Collection, you will find perhaps Luzamba's more politically inclined works, such as his migration series work painted on *Chitenge* (African print) material. Or even his work titled "Strategist," which depicts former Zimbabwean president Robert Mugabe stressing a point with clasped hands. While Mugabe's critics in the West charged him with being a despot accountable for extensive corruption, economic mismanagement, and violations of human rights- especially those pertaining to proponents of same-sex marriage, including racism against white people, and genocide- he is viewed by some like Luzamba as a Pan-Africanist. Muvhuti witnessed this when visiting the SADC capitals, where Mugabe even has streets named after him, or in Namibia's case, a clinic.

During his quest, Muvhuti contacted the reclusive Nelly Guambe in Mozambique, hoping to find out more about a body of work she produced while confined to her flat following her motorbike-related collision with a car. This is an incident that resembles the story of Mexican feminist and surrealist painter Frida Kahlo to a great extent. However, her art is not always as it seems in this series; normally, she paints portraits of women she meets in Maputo's streets. Muvhuti notes that the faces can be interpreted as masks that are concealing a lot, possibly referencing rejection or estrangement.

resembles the story of Mexican feminist and surrealist painter Frida Kahlo to a great extent. However, her art is not always as it seems in this series; normally, she paints portraits of women she meets in Maputo's streets. Muvhuti notes that the faces can be interpreted as masks that are concealing a lot, possibly referencing rejection or estrangement.

All these exciting experiences were made even more memorable by Muvhuti's personal nightmarish encounter of travelling throughout the region on difficult road networks plagued by immigration problems worsened by corruption in some countries.

This is an experience that perhaps made Muvhuti reflect and understand his region more differently and grow an ever-evolving understanding of the territory as well as its art. This brings into mind the person at the centre of the ARAK Collection, its founder, AbdulRahman Al Khulaifi, more familiarly known as A-Rahman, a retired banker. According to Cape Town-based academic, writer, and cultural theorist Ashraf Jamal[7], in 2016, following a 15-day adventure by rail from Dar es Salaam to Cape Town, he developed an irresistible interest in African art. Travelling diagonally from Africa's east coast to its southernmost tip, he, along with his spouse and daughters, passed through Tanzania, Zambia, Zimbabwe, Botswana, and South Africa. But why did A-Rahman become interested in African art, and what was the catalyst for it? It was obvious that the African oddity, its wildlife, or its elegant pastoral scenery did not captivate the collector. However, it turned out to be Africa's aesthetic radioactivity, its instinctive disdain for style, its transformational and disintegrating relationship with raw materials, and its intricate web of both anguish and contentment.

In conclusion, both A-Rahman and Muvhuti's travels serve as a reminder that, despite our sense of unity as a people in this part of Africa known as the SADC region, owing to shared languages, customs, mythologies, and other elements, we are unable to travel freely inside our own territory among its neighbouring nations due to the shameful legacies of colonialism.

[7]Ashraf Jamal, The ARAK Collection, MOL42, Art Times (South Africa).

SECTION ONE

RUDOLF SEIBEB: VISUAL STORYTELLING

THE SETTING

Situated about 70 kilometres to the north of Namibia's capital city of Windhoek is the small city of Okahandja. The two are linked by a smooth dual tarred carriageway characteristic of the sparsely populated nation's state-of-the-art domestic road network, easily seen as one of the finest on the continent of Africa. Okahandja is considered a gateway to the northern coastal areas of the country. In the culture of the Ovaherero and Nama ethnic groups in Namibia, Okahandja is a revered heritage city and the burial place of the former's important royals. Derived from the Otjiherero dialect, the name of the city directly translates to "the place where two rivers (Okakango and Okamita) flow into each other to form one wide one" (Moolman 2015: 14). The city of less than 25,000 inhabitants is also known as the "Garden Town of Namibia."

At the city's south entrance from Windhoek is the Okahandja Mbangura Woodcarvers Craft Market with an assortment of crafts, souvenirs, and other memorabilia. In the market, tucked in the second row and therefore slightly obliterated from the road is artist Rudolf Seibeb's Tadami Khu Arts studio, a shiny structure constructed of corrugated zinc sheets and almost the size and shape of a shipping container. On display outside the studio are some of the artist's finished colourful pieces of different sizes, not far from Ricardo Stramiss' wire cars. Stramiss has worked as Seibeb's assistant for many years. On my visit, he served as our translator, a role he assumes often whenever the artist interacts with visitors speaking to him in English. Seibeb is fluent in his native Damara Nama and Afrikaans, the latter being a language spoken in South Africa and Namibia. Namibia is a former colony of South Africa.

ENCOUNTERING THE ARTIST'S WORK

In the wood market, different craftspeople recycle and upcycle what others discard in the process of woodcarving, jewellery making, beadwork, and other activities taking place on site. It appears a lot is still thrown away, which perhaps explains why the city has gained notoriety for high environmental pollution levels. Although predominantly a painter, Seibeb's practice, which also involves bits of upcycling, thrives in this space where he is spoilt for raw materials. As Frieda Luhl of the Project Room indicates, Seibeb "has always worked with whatever is available, his consistency [with painting] lately has been due to the availability of canvas." The Windhoek based Project Room is the gallery the artist works with. Besides being the source of raw materials, for an artist who is more of a flaneur and a storyteller, the wood market environment is crucial in that it informs the stories the artist transmits to the world. Some of Seibeb's multi-layered media installations build up based on the casual and mundane chats and conversations he has with his neighbours and others from merely observing what is going on around him, his country, and the world in general. He picks up discarded pieces of metal, stone, and other found materials on his walks across the cityscape of Okahandja and its surroundings.

Crammed inside the artist's studio are piles of finished and semifinished works on board and wood, sculpture pieces, a pile of prints, as well as framed certificates of awards won, and newspaper cuttings of stories on the artist and reports of past exhibitions he participated in. The prints lie stacked in the corner. There was no stretched canvas mounted on the easel when I walked in, but containers of paint and brushes were on the table. My initial encounters with Seibeb's work had been via social media on a WhatsApp group of young art collectors from Zimbabwe and secondly, on the ARAK Collection online platform. I had only seen and platform. I had only seen and experienced his pieces from a distance when artist and curator Jo Rogge included him in, *Unmourned Bodies*, an exhibition of Namibian artists at the AVA Gallery in April 2023. Then, Frieda Luhl had shown me a few pieces in storage at the Project Room in Windhoek a day before I travelled to meet the artist.

On the two occasions I stood before the work, I realised that images do not articulate the work well. Besides the distortions that come with the process of capturing, processing, and producing a picture, I also noticed that the artworks sometimes include different multi-layered found materials of all kinds of media concealed on the surfaces. Some of the materials blend well with the canvases or wood backdrop surfaces and the acrylic paints the artist employs in his practice. As such, they would not stand out on an image. In some instances, the materials are painted over as the artist layers the paints and his finds one over the other. Therefore, these aspects of Seibeb's work tend to unveil themselves to the observant naked eye on approach.

PARALLEL AESTHETICS AND TRANSNATIONAL REFERENCES

The presentation of multi-layered images characterised by bold colours and rough brushstrokes in Seibeb's work easily conjure up images of the art of Jean-Michel Basquiat and Abdoulaye Diarrassouba (Aboudia) to audiences with knowledge of art from different parts of the world. While the American-Ivorian artist openly admits that his work is derivative of Basquiat's, it is interesting to note that Seibeb has only heard of the two through audiences who engage with him pointing out the resemblance in the forms, figures, and colours in their respective articulations. Even more interesting is the idea that they all incorporate found objects or unconventional materials in their work. Basquiat left marks on the different media from environments he encountered and felt provided surfaces to draw or paint on. Aboudia enhances his work with newspaper and magazine cut-offs. In the same vein, Seibeb also incorporates wood and metal pieces into his pieces.

While the Namibian artist hardly incorporates text in his work, statements expressed in different fonts and styles are a prominent feature of Basquiat's and Aboudia's works. The influence of graffiti and traditional African masks is clear in Aboudia's work, with Basquiat himself having worked as a graffiti artist in the 1970s. Probably the most distinct common element among the three is the obsession with the detailed oversized human head and face. While Seibeb's heads mainly show detailed faces which the artist seems to employ as gateways to his reading and understanding of society, Basquiat used the oversized skull to try and understand the complicated human mind, and Aboudia tries to capture beautiful emotions on the oversized skulls of children mostly carrying menacing weapons. One can only find out more of these elements when zooming in on the work, whether online or by physically drawing nearer to it. The three artists paint from memory and hardly have any sitters. With the resemblance in the work seemingly clear, how then do we grapple with or accept Seibeb's scanty knowledge of the two? How do we explain the striking similarities in the portrayals of artists whose works he has not encountered before? With the three artists belonging to different Black geographies, is it possible to think of pan-diasporic conversations and connections as a way of linking their practice? These are questions I do not necessarily have answers for. However, what I find distinct in Seibeb's work is the depiction of tall, thin figures, usually women, seen when one zooms in on the face. They are clothed in beautiful black and white, and colourful garments at times, but their thin structures and postures tend to draw me to the sticky figures common in the rock art depictions of the San groups, who are the first peoples and nations of the Southern African region.

In 2003, Seibeb travelled to Zimbabwe, where he participated in the Batapata International Artists Workshop. [8]Batapata was part of a series of workshops known as the, Triangle International Workshops, (commonly referred to as the, Triangle Network.)[9], which were organised locally, but supported by the Triangle Arts Trust founded by Robert Loder (1934-2017) and Antony Caro (1924-2013). In the workshops, artists and practitioners focused on crafts and visual media for two to three weeks, sharing ideas and critiquing each other's work and practice. For Seibeb, attending the event was eye-opening in more than one way. As the artist reflected in our conversation, he witnessed and listened to testimonies of people living off their art and craft. In other words, he realised one could be sustained by a career in the arts. He also encountered Zimbabwe's stone sculptors and found the way some of the artists worked with stone and different media quite astounding. Seibeb talks of an artist who combined stone, wood, and shoes in his pieces, for example. He could have encountered Tapfuma Gutsa, whose practice is quite experimental and is credited for transforming Zimbabwe's reductive stone sculpture tradition in profound ways. Gutsa participated in almost all the Triangle Network workshops in Zimbabwe over the years. Even more surprising to Seibeb was the presence of female sculptors patiently using hand tools to sculpt stone. The artist states that attending the Batapata Workshop transformed his practice.

[8]Batapata was an offshoot of the Pachipamwe International Artits Workshop, founded by Pat Pearce and sponsored by The Triangle Network. Pachipamwe I took place in Murehwa in 1988 and Pachipamwe II was held at Cyrene Mission in 1989 (See footnote 9 below).

[9] As highlighted by Hayden Proud in the Five Bhobh exhibition catalogue, "The Triangle Network" (also called the Triangle Arts Trust) is a registered charitable organisation in Britain. It has supported and fostered collaborations involving artists from grassroots organisations in different countries around the world since 1982. It also supported the Thupelo Workshops first initiated by David Koloane and Bill Ainslie in Johannesburg in 1985"(2019: 92). In Namibia's case, the Triangle Network supported two editions of the Tulipamwe International Artists Workshop in 2001 and 2003.

APPROPRIATED OBJECTS AND ASSEMBLAGES

At this juncture, I look at selected works by Seibeb in the ARAK Collection. I am interested in their appearance and material composition. I also try to go at length to offer my reading of the work. However, I am not saying my reading of the work is the only way the work should be understood, as art interpretation is always subjective.

When Visiting Cape Town (2022) is a three-dimensional work painted at the height of the COVID-19 pandemic. However, at the time the painting was done, the World Health Organisation (WHO) and respective governments all over the world had relaxed the lockdown regulations and people were traveling again. Dominating the frame is a long, wooden boat with a cabin plastered with clay and painted green on top. Instead of the traditional mast with discernible sails, the boat has two wooden masts linked together by a rolled fabric. One of the masts is painted white. Of the two wooden stock anchors at the far ends of the boat, one lies on the surface of the surrounding water body while the other serves as the long nose of a figure's face in the bottom-left corner. They are tied to the boat using a thread cut from a tyre and a shoelace. The animals depicted in the centre could be springboks. Belonging to the buck family and found throughout the veldts of the Southern African region, springboks are popular in South Africa, where their icon serves as the emblem of the national rugby team. Easily noticeable is how one animal's belly playfully doubles as the mouth of the largest of the three portraits anchored on the boat. Of the four main faces in the frame, two are smiling as their teeth are on display and two seem to be serious with closed mouths. These facial expressions can be read as the artist's expression of mixed emotions and uncertainty at the time the painting was made. The world was not certain of whether the pandemic was behind us, or whether it would live with us for eternity.

As per the artist's trademark way of incorporating found materials in his frames, the wood boat, cabin, masts, anchors, threads, and the behind us, or whether it would live with us for eternity. As per the artist's trademark way of incorporating found materials in his frames, the wood boat, cabin, masts, anchors, threads, and the fabric are the 'surprise' elements included in this work. Counting the heads alone, I seem to find seventeen humans in the piece as the artist squeezes in full figures inside the portraits and other portraits in-between the main ones. Read in another way, all that is anchored on the boat appears like a huge island floating on the sea, and the face in the bottom left as the smaller island with its own activities going on. Painted from the artist's memory, the work could have been his way of celebrating that people could travel again. What nearest place could he have in mind than the majestic Cape Town?

“Seibeb does not shy away from engaging the key contentious and sensitive topics in the politics of Africa’s south-western state.”

Also painted at the height of the pandemic are *People Happy Amid Covid-19* (2022) and *People and the Domestic Animals in Place* (2022). Descendible in the former are two broad faces. One of them appears like a colourful mural on the wall while the other serves as the belly of a tall, thin figure. Just like in all the paintings he produced at the period of the pandemic, what fascinates me the most is the carefree attitude of the subjects as is signified by the absence of the mask, the aesthetic of the pandemic. In the latter, one sees the elephant, donkey, and duck juxtaposed with the people in the same frame. By dissolving the assumed borders between humans and animals in the work, the artist seems to be acknowledging how the animals came out and roamed freely, sometimes into areas that human beings had restricted them from wandering into. It is his way of acknowledging their freedom at the time human beings were confined to their domestic spaces, paying heed to the restrictions imposed by the WHO and their respective governments. According to Frieda Luhl, "His strong connection to nature, symbolized by recurring animal motifs, reflects his wish for a peaceful coexistence and harmony." In other words, in some of his works, Seibeb stresses our kinship with the environment.

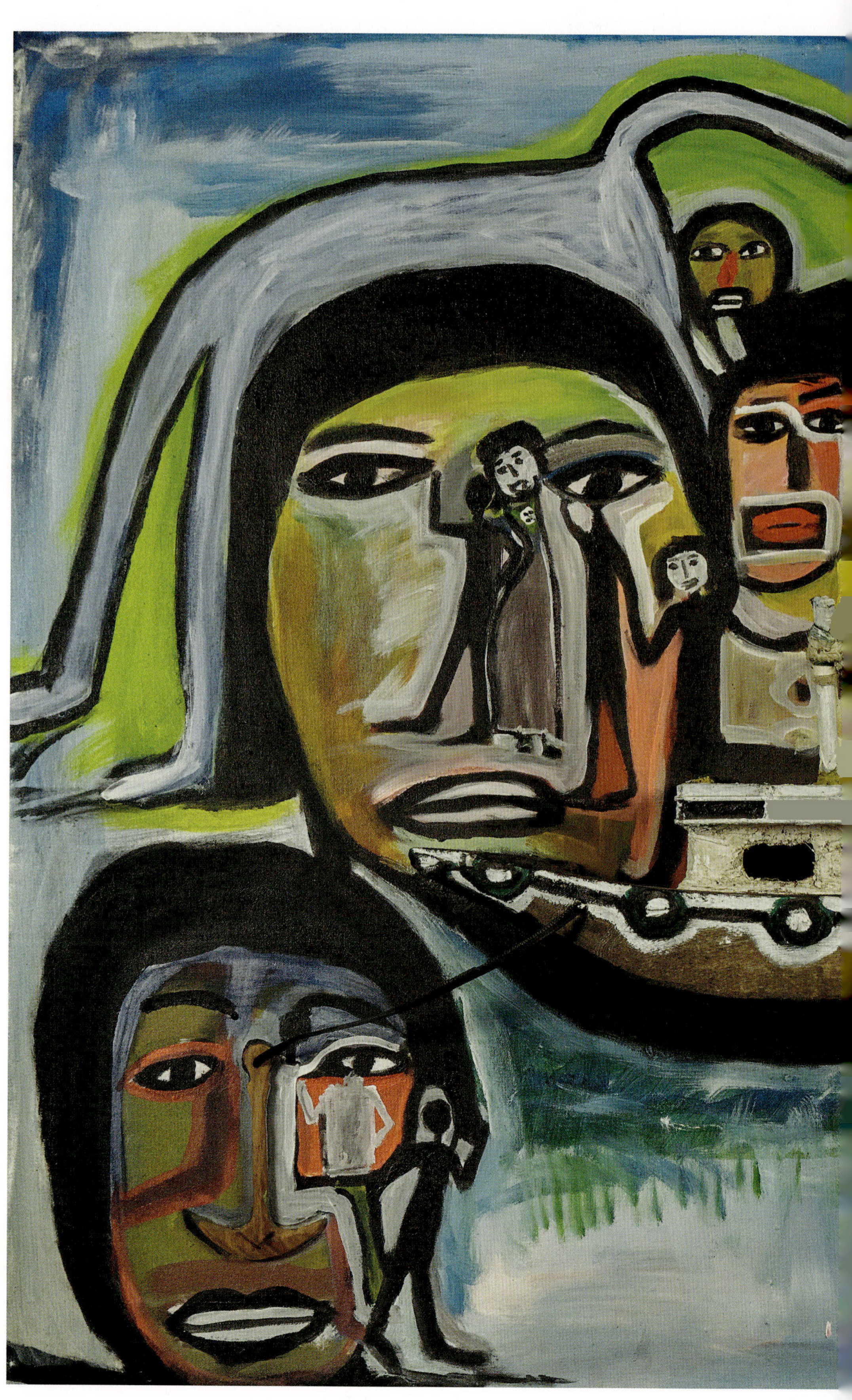

When Visiting Cape Town | Rudolf Seibeb
2022 | 91cm x 119cm | Acrylic on canvas

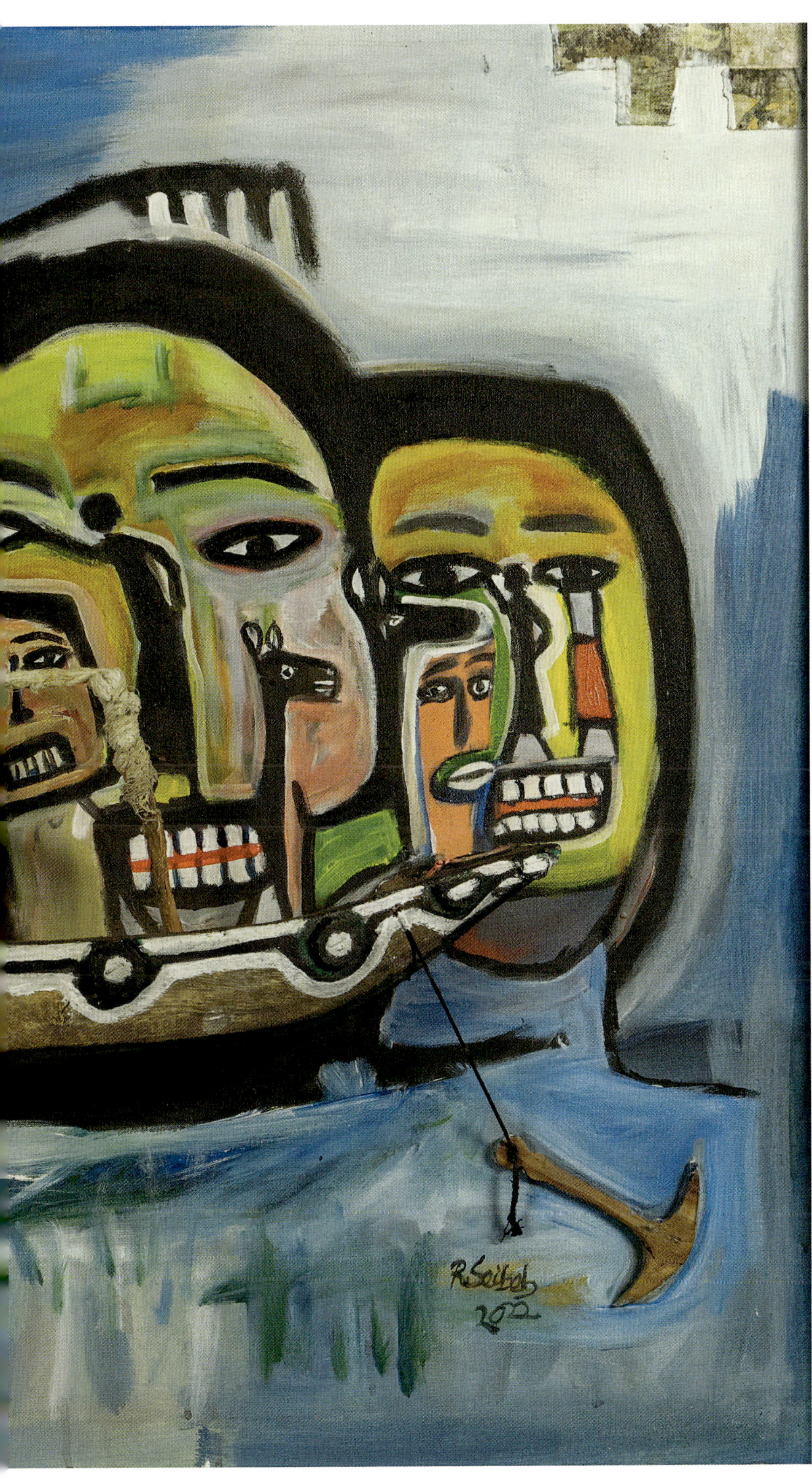

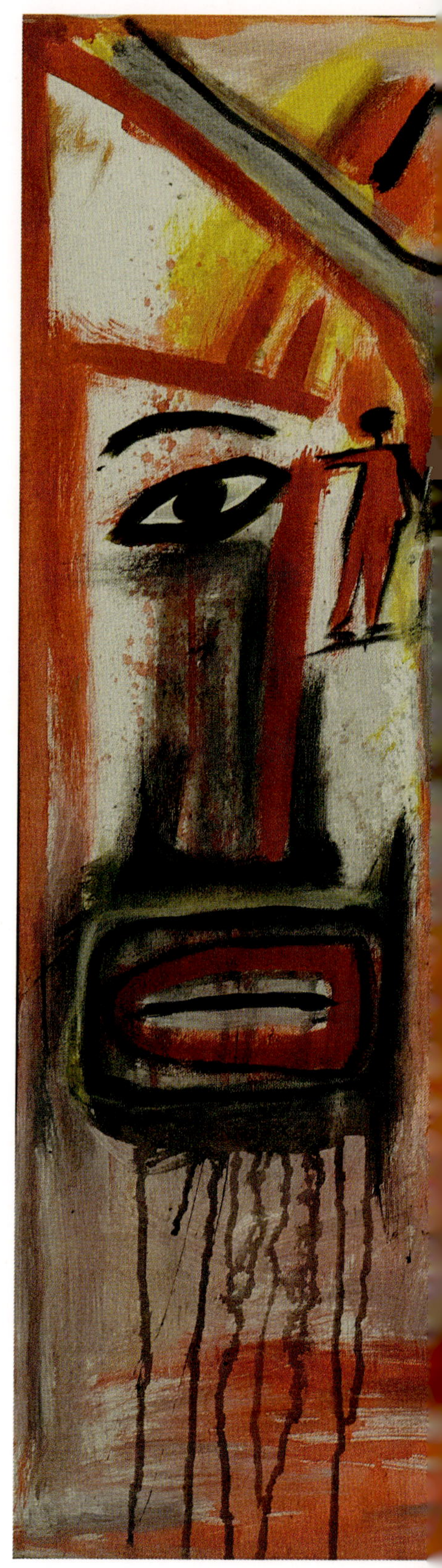

People Happy Amid Covid-19 | Rudolf Seibeb
2022 | 77cm x 98cm | Acrylic on canvas

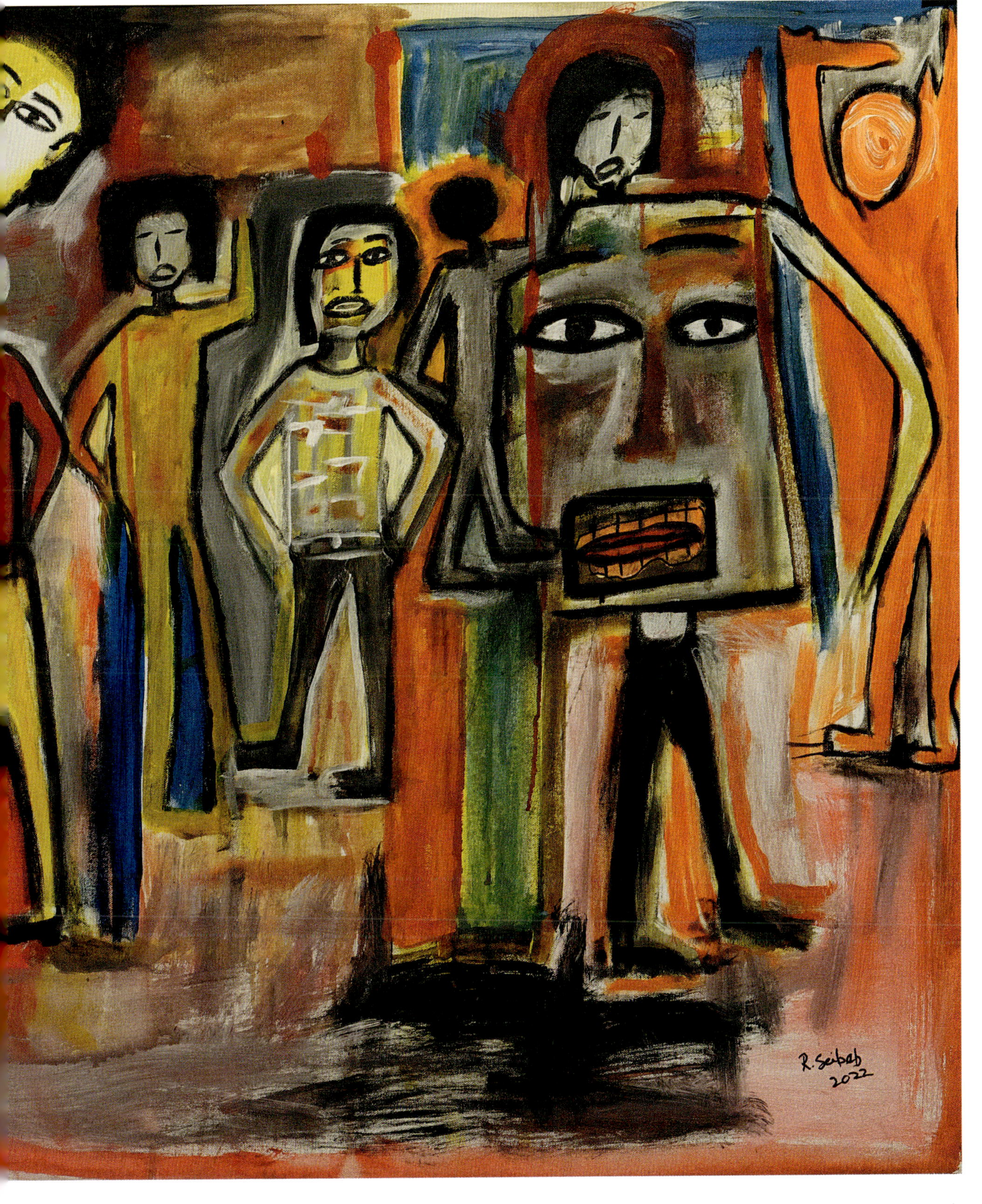
R. Seibab
2022

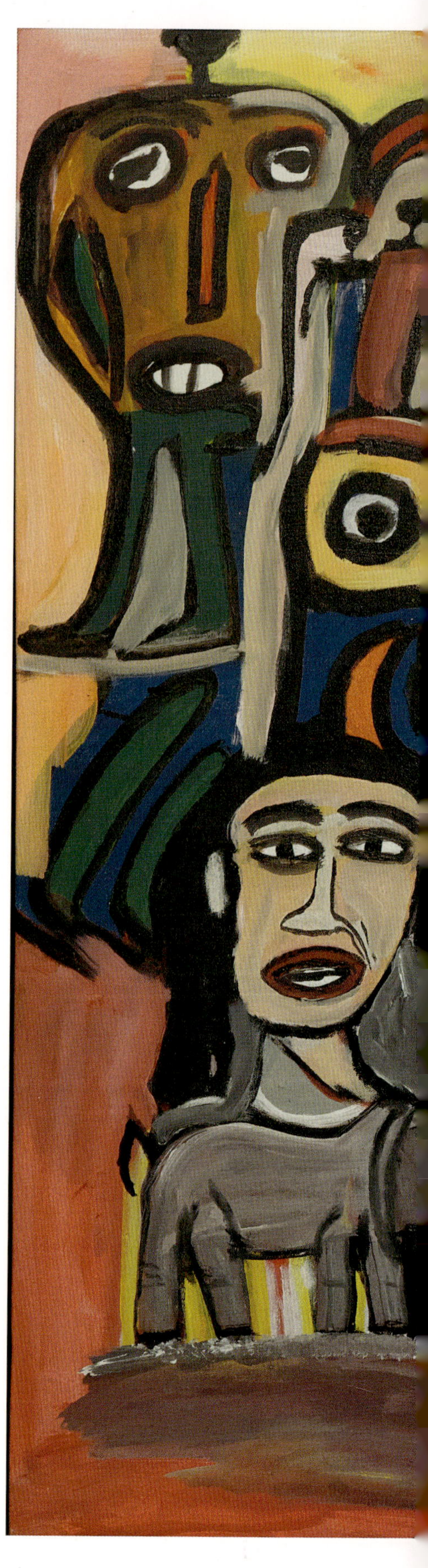

People and Domestic Animals in Peace | Rudolf Seibeb
2022 | 93cm x 101cm | Acrylic on canvas

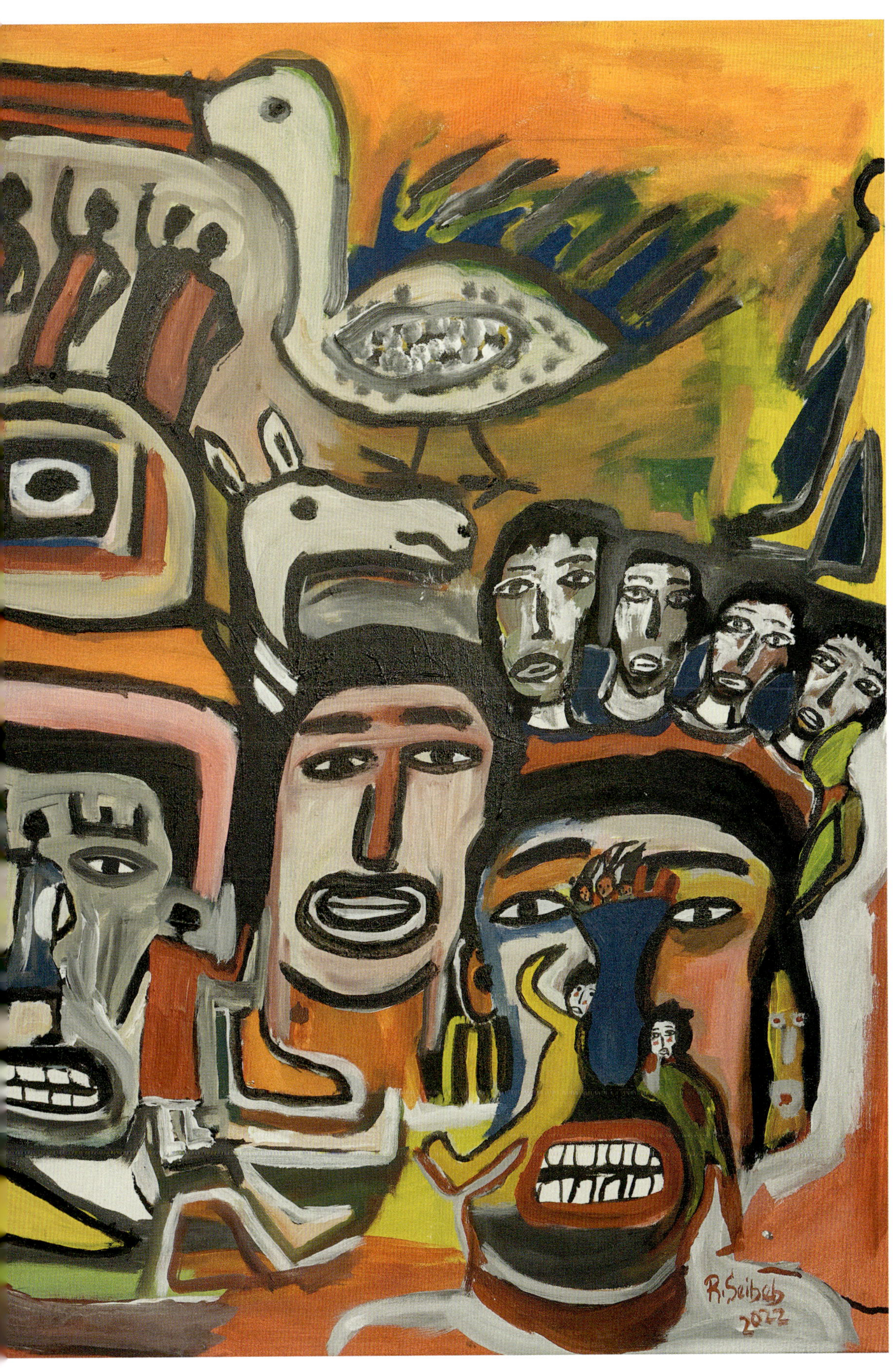

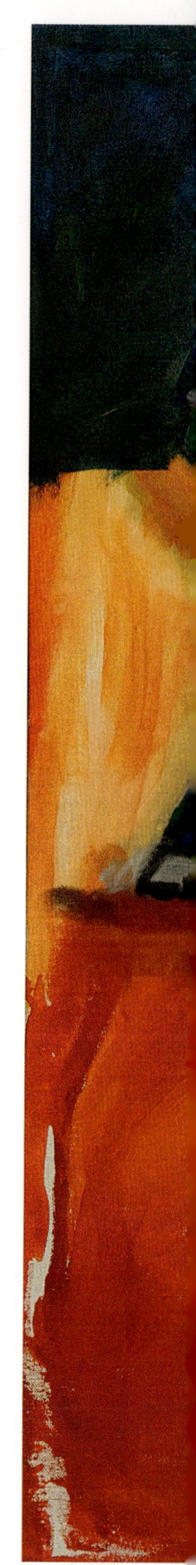

People Conscious About Speaking Out | Rudolf Seibeb
2022 | 81cm x 91cm | Acrylic on canvas

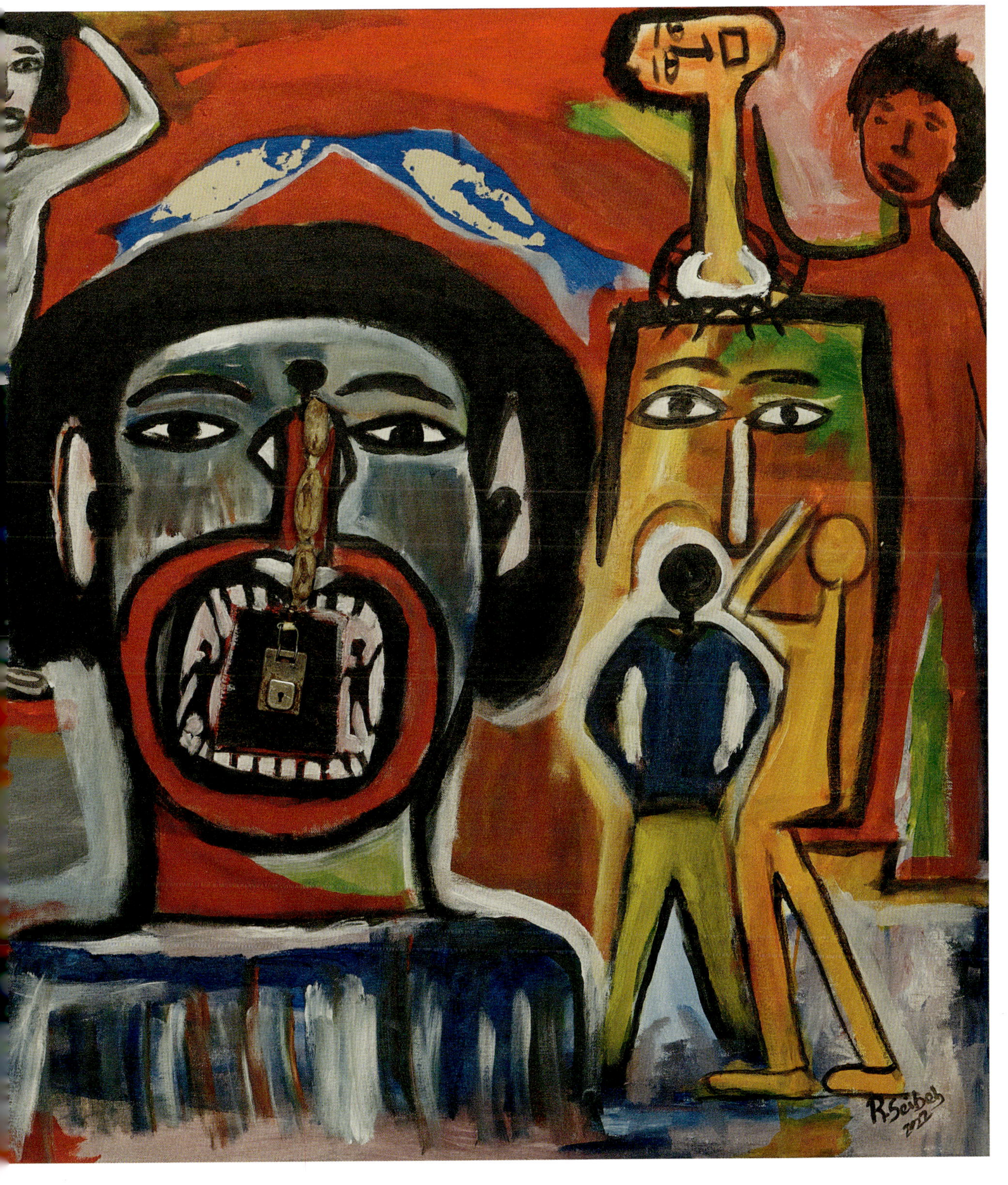
R.Seibeh
2022

“If artists are expected to assume a distinctive style, then Siebeb has done so highly effectively. His paintings, given time and greater exposure, will prove iconic.”

-Ashraf Jamal

People Conscious About Speaking Out (2022) is an artwork which demonstrates that Seibeb does not shy away from engaging the key contentious and sensitive topics in the politics of Africa's south-western state. In what has been dubbed the 'Fishrot case,' individual key figures in the Ministry of Fisheries were singled out for cutting under-the-table deals with an Icelandic fishing company named Samherji. The individuals, who included the Minister of Fisheries at the time, were alleged to have accepted millions of dollars in bribes (quota fees) in exchange for fishing quotas off the country's coast. Although the investigation process took years, the publication of the findings in 2019 resulted in the resignation of high-level officials, including Minister of Fisheries Bernhard Esau and the Minister of Justice Sacky Shanghala, with both being indicted for corruption, fraud, and money laundering by the Namibian authorities. It is this case that is the subject of this work by Seibeb. In the centre of the frame is a figure who appears to be shouting. Above the head of the figure are two fish seemingly swimming towards each other. The bust of the central figure is a body of water in the same blue colour as the water the fish are swimming in. Two figures in the frame adopt interesting standing postures. The one to the top-left corner has his hand on his head, while the one with a yellow bottom and a blue shirt in the bottom-right corner has hands on his waist. The two's postures suggest that they are shocked by the unfolding events. So is the yellow figure in the bottom-right corner. The red figure in the top-right corner is hoisting a puppet-like figure, perhaps in the mould of Conrad Koch's Chester Messing, notorious for his sarcastic take on serious and scandalous political matters in neighbouring South Africa. I am drawn to the depiction of the puppet's elongated neck in a similar style to figures produced by the Cameroonian artist Joël Mpah Dooh or the Senegalese modernist Ibrahima Kébé. This can be read as evidence of parallel aesthetics across different locations on the continent.

Zooming into the centre of the piece, we find a padlock inside the open mouth of the shouting central figure. Seibeb shrewdly placed it in its position to make a statement that speaking out is key if people want to hold state officials accountable to avoid being short-changed by their own governments. On both sides of the padlock, two black figures appear to be sloganeering confidently. What appears like a padlock holder extending as the nose of the central figure are three joined silk moth cocoons. The shaman dancers of Botswana insert seeds inside the cocoons (locally known as Matlhoa) and tie them around their ankles to produce a coordinated rattling sound when dancing. The use of this found material by Seibeb can also be read as a metaphor for the power of speaking in unison.

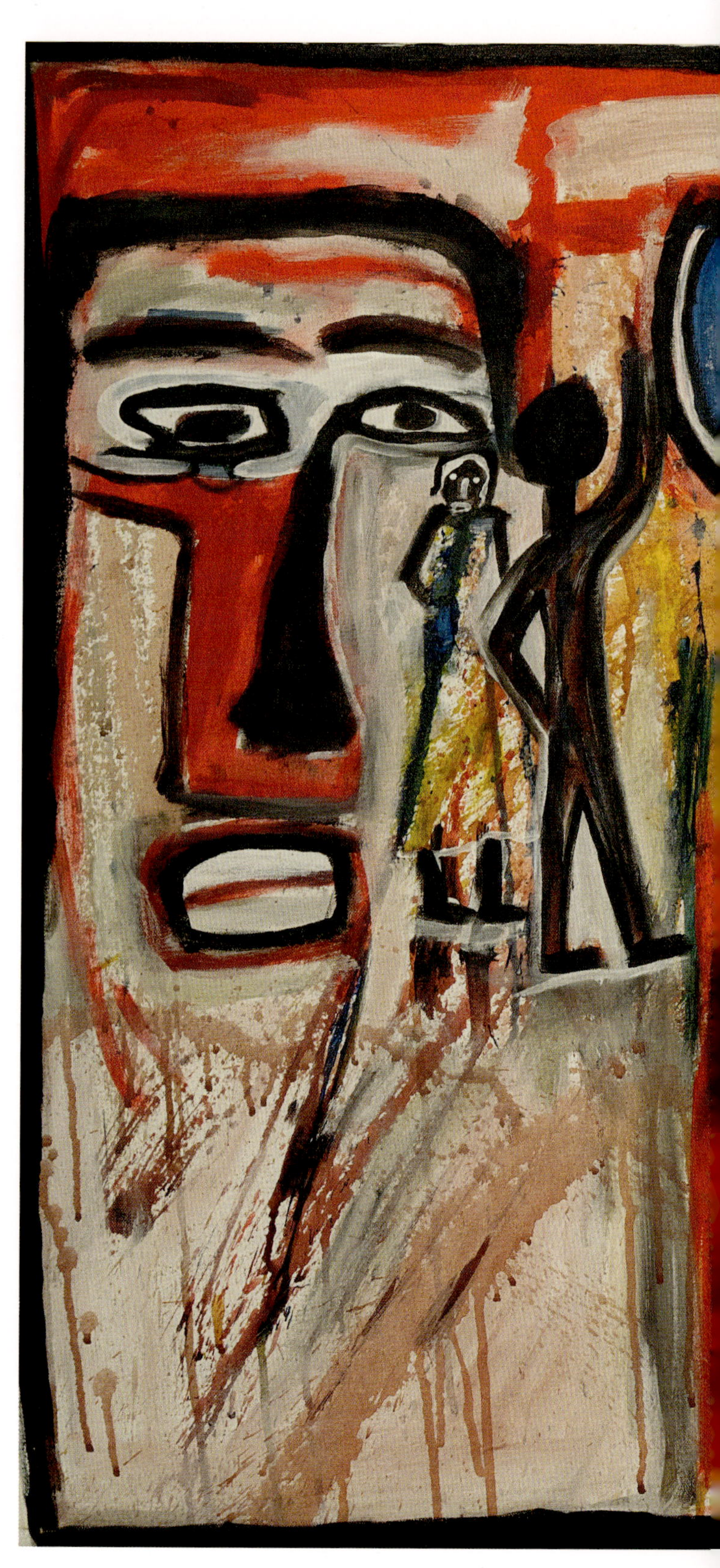

Democracy in Progress | Rudolf Seibeb
2022 | 77cm x 98cm | Acrylic on canvas

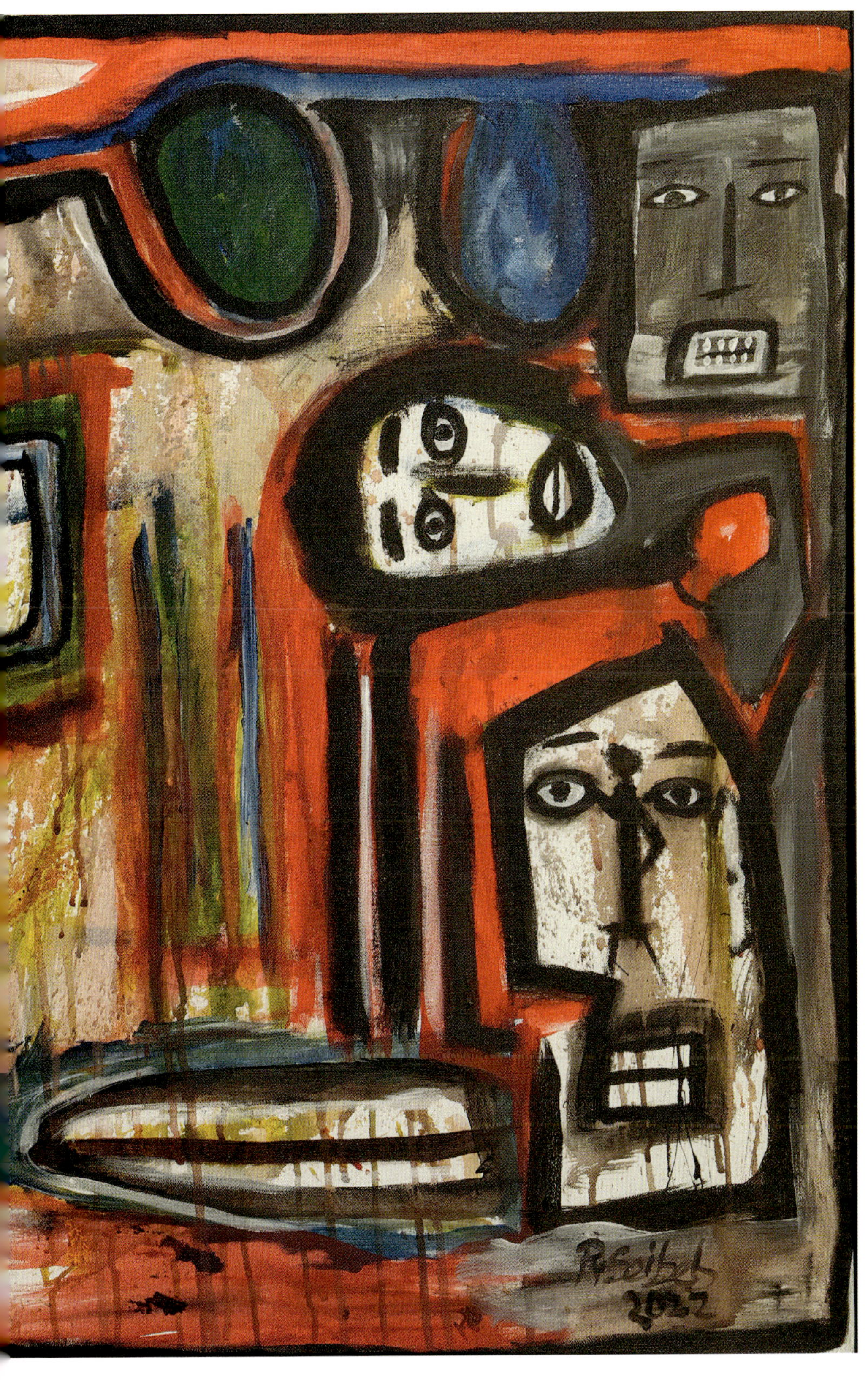

The message in the work resonates with the people in neighbouring Southern African countries that have been affected by unprecedented levels of corruption, especially those that are still run by liberation war movements, which have turned out to be some of the world's most corrupt political formations and mafias. After exposing the corruption in Namibia in a documentary titled *Anatomy of the Bribe* in 2020, the Qatari state-owned Al Jazeera Media Network went on to publish the rot in Zimbabwe in the Gold Mafia documentary produced in 2023. Endemic corruption is also crippling the African National Congress-led South Africa, and so is the case with Mozambique under the ruling FRELIMO party. Due to its expository nature, the work can be read as protest art, which is generally not meant to be enjoyed. However, unlike a confrontational artist like South Africa's Ayanda Mabulu, for example, Seibeb has found a subtle way of engaging heated political matters employing coded language and symbols.

Democracy in Progress (2022) is one of the works Seibeb also produced during the pandemic. While the title appears like the artist is appreciative of the developments in Namibia or anywhere on the continent regarding progress on the political terrain, certain aspects of the work suggest he is quite sceptical about it. Firstly, what appears like a pair of glasses at the top and the big eye in the centre suggest the masses are always under surveillance from the state, in Orwellian fashion, of course! Unlike other paintings by the same artist, which are tidied up, albeit with visible rough brushstrokes, red and dark paints are left dripping over the surface of the painting. By presenting them like that, perhaps the artist is reminding us that in parts of Africa, the road to democracy is always messy as it involves the shedding of blood, sweat, and tears. In African countries, democracy comes at a price.

Traditional Way of Treating Illness in the Village (2020) is a work the artist also painted during the pandemic. The figures in it stand against a multicoloured background. The figure with dreadlocks could be the Sangoma or shaman as its body is transformed into something that is not clearly definable and mysterious. The two figures in yellow and red could be the ones consulting the healer. The ghostly figure to the left seems to belong to the spiritual world. The figures have no masks. Through the work, the artist could be reminding the world that Africans turned to remedies at a time the pandemic was expected to ravage the continent the hardest as it is known for its deteriorating medical facilities and infrastructure.

With an almost monochromatic backdrop, *Victims of social evil* (2018) is an earlier painting by Seibeb. What quickly draws one's attention is the head which sits on top of the other, bayonetted by five swords. Its dripping blood flows around the two heads below it. While the four main heads depicted in the artwork are painted in a similar form, we are accustomed to seeing in the artist's work, especially from the latter years, that his lines are thin. The figures' eyes seem to be looking past the viewer, in the manner of one contemplating or just absent-minded. There is emptiness in their gazes. With the signage on them, the bottle squeezed in-between the heads, and the one to the far right are not placed there by chance. One carries the symbol of the Acquired Immuno-Deficiency Syndrome (AIDS) scourge, which has ravaged some parts of the continent and the other depicts a seemingly immoral social scene, one that may lead to the spread of the disease. The presence of the bottles seems to be the artist's coded message that people tend to behave irresponsibly when under the influence of alcohol. It strikes me as an artwork that refuses to be enjoyed as it is meant to educate society or raise awareness of the scourge. The artist does not go for the spectacle but engages the uncomfortable subject.

Among the multiple media Seibeb works in is printmaking. *Africa's People Unite for Poverty* (2022) is a complex artwork with pronounced patterns. The main figure appears like a face with twisted calabashes as its eyes. The calabashes have defined facial features of their own, with the mouths and eyes standing out. Taking the form and shape of a nose is a standing woman. What I find fascinating about this work are the patterns known in African architecture and fabrics. There is a bit of cross-hatching, the checker designs, as well as the chevrons, and many others. Printmaking is not a new art form on the Namibian art scene, with John Ndevasia Muafangejo, who is probably the Southern African nation's most famous artist, having been a printmaker.

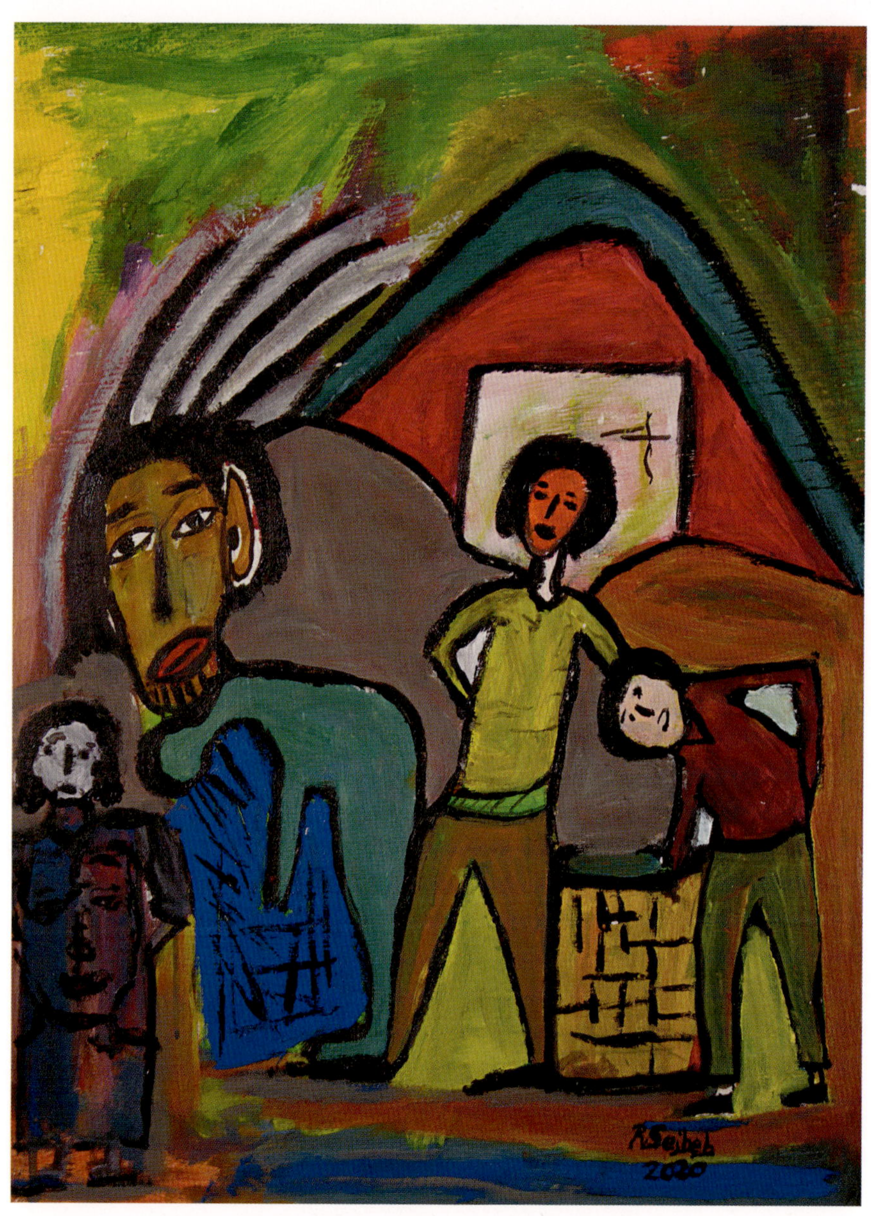

Traditional way of treating illness in the village | Rudolf Seibeb
2020 | 60cm x 45 cm | Acrylic on board

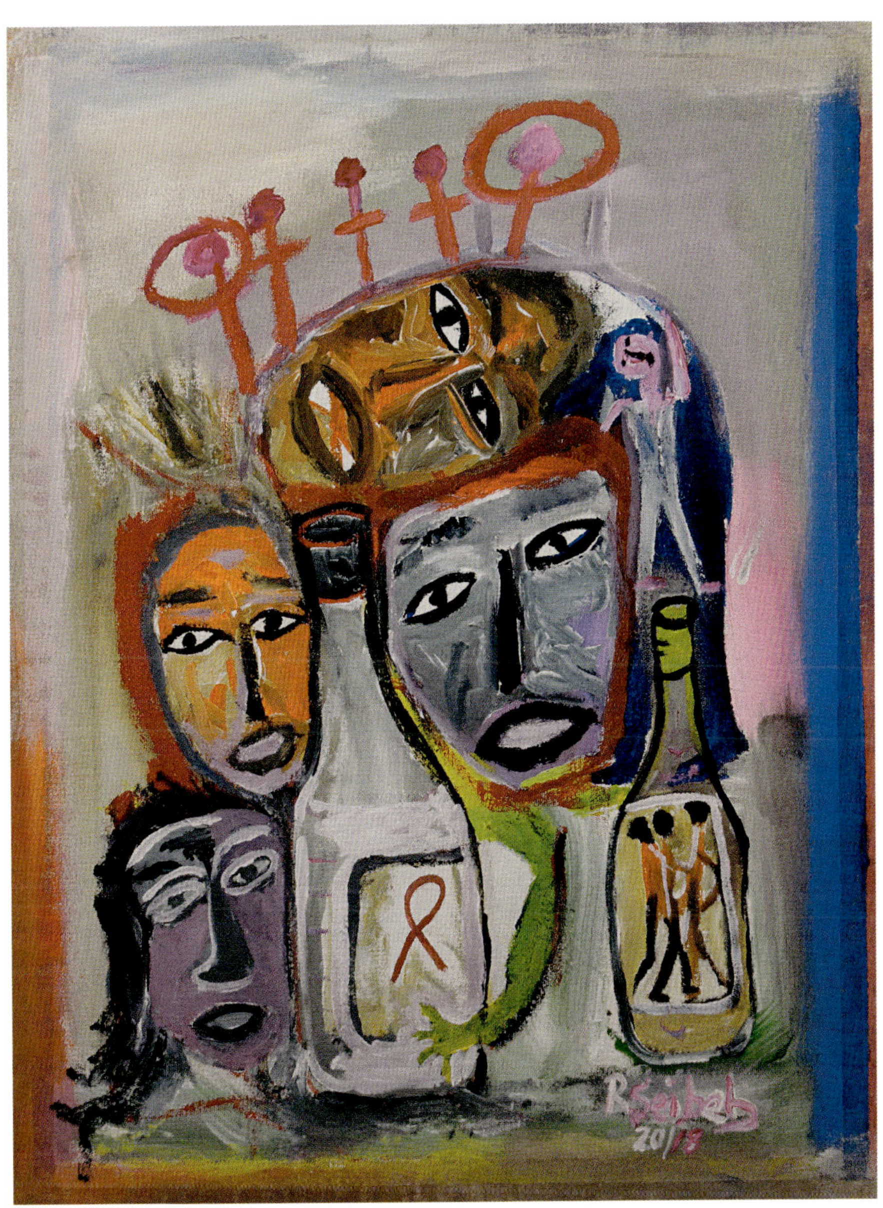

Victims of social evil | Rudolf Seibeb
2018 | 60cm x 45.6cm | Acrylic on canvas

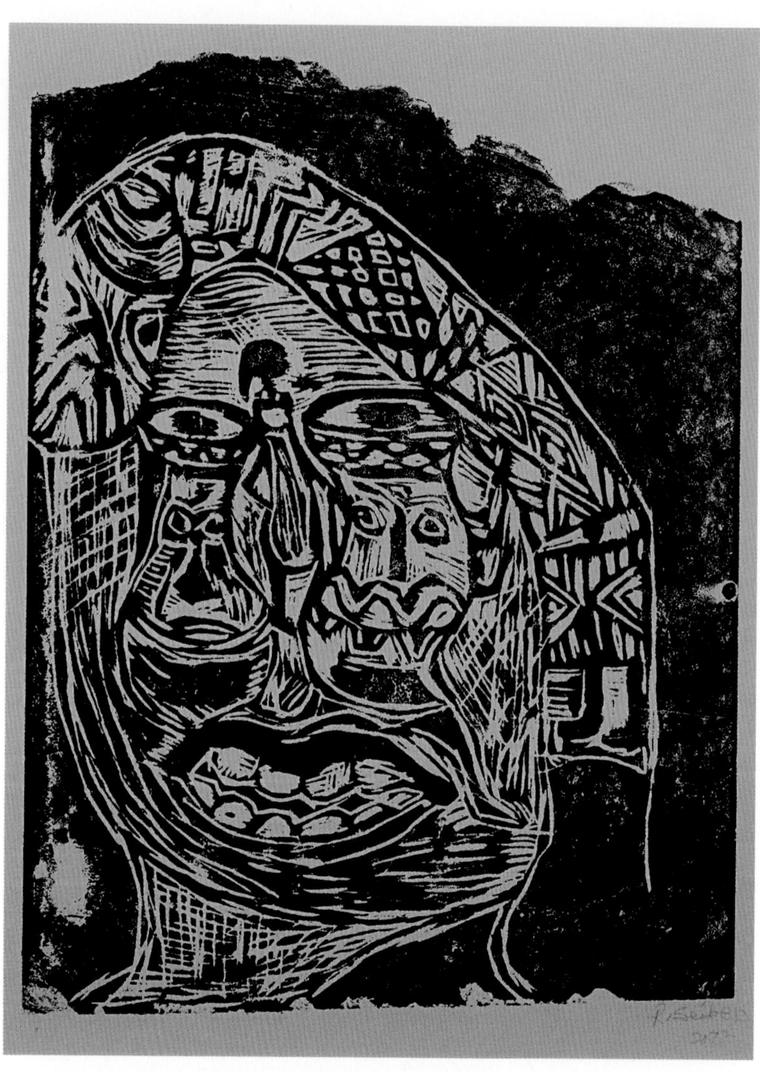

Africa's People Unite for Poverty | Rudolf Seibeb
2022 | 50cm x 38cm | Pastel on paper

INSIGHTS FROM NAMIBIA

Reading through the oft-duplicated biographical information on Seibeb, we learn that he is an autodidact or self-taught artist, and yet elsewhere, we also learn that he was one of the first artists to attend the John Muafangejo Art Centre at the time it was established in 1994.

According to Jo Rogge, who mentored Seibeb at the time, the school's curriculum revolved around printmaking, drawing, and sculpture. Artists made use of resources like cardboard and wood in their craft. Screen-printing was also a feature of the curriculum. The centre was established to impart skills and empower a generation of mostly aspiring artists from marginalised backgrounds, hoping that they would earn income to sustain their lives. Seibeb was already a practising artist when he enrolled at the centre. As Frieda Luhl highlights:

Seibeb emerged from humble beginnings, armed with sheer determination and a modest budget. He transformed found objects into art pieces that echoed his vivid imagination. It was the encouragement from fellow artist Shiya Karuseb that paved Rudolf's path to the John Muafangejo Art Centre in Windhoek. Under the mentorship of Shiya Karuseb, Kay Cowley, Erik Schnack, Helena Brandt and Jo Rogge and amidst formal training, Rudolf's raw talent blossomed.

Rogge, who taught at the centre, emphasises that what transpired at the institution was more of an exchange of ideas with the mentors also learning from mentees. This seems like a characteristic trait of the early art schools and workshops in the Southern African region as it also happened much earlier at the Polly Street Art Centre in Johannesburg in the 1950s and 1960s, for example, where the artistic practice of the mentor Cecil Skotnes transformed to incorporate African themes, styles, and motifs as he started working with the South African modernist sculptor Sydney Kumalo and many other Black artists. Although there was a lot of experimentation with new techniques at the institution, Rogge emphasises that what mostly shifted in Seibeb's practice at the time was him becoming assured that what he was doing was fine. In illustrating this sentiment, Rogge drops a few names of artists from Namibia who emerged from the school, travelled abroad where they experimented with different materials and forms, only to come back to a nation where they had lost recognition due to their lack of consistency. Rogge argues that Seibeb's consistency separates him from the rest of the artists. It has made him the mainstay of Namibia's mainstream canon for long.

Ndeenda Shivute-Nakapunda, the chief curator of the National Art Gallery of Namibia (NAGN), recently included Seibeb in *An ODE to the MASTERS*, an exhibition at the NAGN in March and April of 2023. She indicated that Seibeb's artworks are unique in terms of form and appearance, and anyone can easily identify the style. However, when it comes to the process of making them, Shivute-Nakapunda argues that the artist's "assemblages" are characteristic of the Namibian art scene, where different local artists work with found materials, which they mostly incorporate or layer in their sculptural works. While she recognises the fact that Seibeb has been at the centre of the Namibian art scene for a while, she laments that he only earned recognition much later in his practice. As such, she finds it difficult to classify him as the artist bridging the gap between the nation's modern and contemporary scenes.

Frieda Luhl elaborates that Seibeb has a "distinct signature that is visible consistently in his paintings, drawings, prints and sculptures." She indicates that his work's inclusion in the ARAK Collection signifies not only his talent but also the importance of his narratives. "Rudolf's art is a reflection of his world—a tapestry of faces, emotions, and narratives intertwined with the fabric of his community... Through his works, he confronts pressing issues, drawing inspiration from both local and global events, resonating with audiences far and wide." Luhl cites his two solo exhibitions, *Hokverhale/Navigating a Lockdown* and the evocative *Mens(gemaak)* as thought-provoking shows, which helped affirm "his versatility and depth, catching the discerning eyes of many within the Namibian art scene."

CONCLUSION

At the centre of Seibeb's work are large human faces depicting diversity across race and background. They are humanity's most common recognisable element. In the artist's work, there are always other activities and motions unfolding within the broader face. One discovers these on approaching the work. Drawing from his surroundings and across the region, through his practice, Seibeb tells local stories the way a flâneur and documentarist would. His practice is enriched by transnational references and elements, mostly from Southern Africa. The found materials he upcycles have had a full life cycle of their own, bearing witness to the daily lives of the people around him. Thus, with their use, Seibeb provides a visual map and archive of a life that was, and we try to figure it out whenever we fix our eyes on the object. However, like in the work of any other conceptual artist applying fresh thoughts to the work, the meaning of the objects shifts based on the narrative the artist is putting across. Spending time locally and within the craft market allows the artist to expand the field of painting by incorporating the diverse materials at his disposal. By incorporating these elements, he is upcycling and adding value to what would have been discarded and polluting the environment. While the city of Okahandja where he operates from is detached from the centre of Namibia's capital city and the centre of the country's art scene, it is a place rich in the materials the artist uses and feeds the narratives he transmits. Thus, the incorporated materials also embody local experiences. The artist highlights that there are no distractions in the relatively quiet Okahandja, where he concentrates on his work and finds time to spend with the guests who visit his Tadami Khu Arts studio.

SECTION TWO

THEBE PHETOGO: REIMAGINING LOCAL MYTHS

A VISIT TO MATSIENG

At sunset on Thursday the 27th of July, Tumelo Lekolwane and I arrived at the small building which serves as the reception centre for local and international tourists visiting the site of Matsieng Footprints. I immediately noticed a car parked about ten metres to the right of the building. Placed on the ground next to it were three transparent five-litre containers filled with what looked like a contaminated greenish liquid. My stare at the containers was interrupted by the custodian of the site, who came out to welcome us. He immediately started to brief us on what we were about to encounter. While we were talking to him, three men joined us. They looked disinterested in all the information being shared with us. As such, the custodian waved them to proceed ahead of us. With the way they did not even ask any questions and for directions, we could tell they knew exactly where to go. This was not their first time at the site.

When we eventually followed them to the site, we noticed that two of them were ferrying water to a nearby bush, where they were pouring it onto their semi-naked bodies. The third one was praying separate from the others. Not only were the two soaking their bodies in the water, but they were also drinking it. They also carried some of the water to the parking spot, where we saw them spraying it on their car. The custodian told us that they would mix some of the water they were taking home with tap water and use it for domestic purposes.

What we had just witnessed appeared like a piece of performance live art, yet it was a cleansing ritual, where the participants were supposedly washing away their burdens. That is what happens often at the revered site of Matsieng. The place is a living heritage site considered a sacred space in the history of sections of Batswana society. As the custodian emphasised, the site attracted both local and international visitors coming to partake in rituals of different kinds. Some of the visitors are said to be coming from as far beyond the continent of Africa as China and India.

Matsieng Footprints is a 30-minute drive from Gaborone, located just after Rosesa Village. It is the site of an expansive undulating rock mass with numerous deep crevices, with the deepest and widest one occupying the centre. Whether they are engravings left by the early foraging Stone Age San communities or are random mysterious formations, there are indeed what appears like footprints of humans and animals on the surface. Among them is a giant one believed to have been that of Matsieng, who is said to have been the servant of Lowe, the ancestor of the Batswana. As Ellenberger (1972: 135) explains:

Legend has it that Lowe, who lived in a cavern under the rock, sent Matsieng outside to see what sort of place the outer world was and that when he returned and told his master that it was a fine place, full of game, trees and grass, Lowe liberated the baTswana and told them to go out and people the earth.

The animal petroglyphs have also been explained as those of the creatures that emerged out of the cave following him. I also learned that Matsieng is not the only site revered in local traditions. Another one in Botswana exists in Maokagane in Kopong, and the other one in Madimatle Mountain in the Limpopo Province in South Africa. As Thebe Phetogo indicates in his Master of Fine Art thesis, the three sites have transnational ties and therefore the potential to unite the people who uphold the myths associated with them. To me, it is a case of communities with cultural ties that were torn apart by the establishment of colonial boundaries. It is unfortunate that the 'liberated' states we have today still uphold the colonial demarcations.

Without the myths ascribed to it, nothing much is spectacular about the site of Matsieng Footprints. However, that the Batswana and those from far away places continue to believe in the myths associated with the site is not strange or unique to them as it is human trait, well summed up by the philosopher Yuval Noah Harari (Gabbai 2015) when he says:

All other animals use their communication system only to describe reality. A chimpanzee may say, look, there is a banana tree over there, let's go and get bananas. Humans, in contrast, use their language not merely to describe reality but also to create new realities, fictional realities.

The said "new realities" and "fictional realities" are some of the pillars binding humanity together. Interestingly, it is the imagination of this site and the others related to it within the grand narrative of his nation that Motswana artist Phetogo plays around with, employing its precolonial narrative to contest the prevailing narrative of how Botswana came to be. As he highlights in his thesis, "the basis for the content of my paintings draws from the wellspring of myths associated with the origination of the Republic of Botswana in 1966" (Phetogo 2019: 8). In doing so, the artist is opening space for the nationals of Botswana to rethink some of the national histories they have internalised, which are created and reinforced by the government through national symbols.

CONTEXT OF THE DOMINANT NARRATIVE

The mainstream narrative for the creation of Botswana that the artist cites is that of three chiefs, namely Khama, Bathoen, and Sebele, who are said to have travelled to the United Kingdom in 1895 to meet the queen and to seek British protection so that their country would not be taken over by Cecil John Rhodes and the British South Africa Company. The advantage of having the protectorate status at the time is not very clear because their territory remained the passage through which the company connected the territories it had annexed in present-day Zimbabwe and Zambia, with the Cape. Moreover, it is even more interesting when one considers that the Rudd Concession of 1888, which paved the way for the colonisation of present-day Zimbabwe, indicated that the company would be occupying and running the territory on behalf of the queen. Considering that the company was a business entity in pursuit of profits, could it not be the case that they had not discovered any interesting resource in the then Bechuanaland and were therefore not that interested in occupying it? This also makes sense when one considers that the occupation of Matabeleland was so brutal that it involved a war, meaning Cecil John Rhodes could do whatever it took to annex a territory he desired.

The story of the three chiefs has been used to shape Motswana identity. It is enshrined in the story of the nation, and it is emphasised through the Botswana Television (BTV) broadcasts. Moreover, it is also taught in schools. As the artist argues in his thesis, the narrative has also become the pillar of the Botswana Democratic Party, which has been in power since the attainment of independence. At some point, the country's president was Ian Khama, a descendent of one of the chiefs. The narrative has even been used to explain the peaceful transitions, which has been the case each time a leader takes over the reign from a predecessor, albeit Ian Khama, who is now living in exile due to bad blood between him and Mokgweetsi Masisi, his successor, who is the incumbent president. The idea of the artist deriving his paintings from the site of Matsieng is to draw the people's attention to the alternative precolonial narrative(s) to make people reflect on what he perceives as the presence of "the colonial hand in the writing of the narrative of Botswana" (Phetogo 2016: 10). It is a story he thinks should be taught at the formative level as compared to the narrative the government advances.

REFLECTIONS FROM A DISTANCE

Phetogo's temporary relocation to South Africa in pursuit of a Fine Art education coincided with an interesting period in the history of tertiary education in the country. In 2015, students at the University of Cape Town embarked on a decolonisation drive in which they demanded the removal of the statue of the British arch-imperialist Cecil John Rhodes as a symbolic gesture of the actual transformation they needed to see reflected in their curricula, the staff of the university and the student intake, among an array of other demands. Phetogo had enrolled at the Michaelis School of Fine Arts, which is the UCT's art campus. This means he found himself at the epicentre of the decolonisation drive, which quickly spread to other universities in the country like 'bushfire in the harmattan,' to borrow Chinua Achebe's phrase.

The distance away from home gave Phetogo time to reflect and to question the notion of culture as fixed or unchanging in his country of birth, as he sees it as a hybrid object informed by a diversity of aspects and elements. He started to critically look at how Botswana had negotiated and constructed their postcolonial identity, building on an "imaginary world" centred on national myths. It was in that period that he started working on a body of work, which is more of his own imaginary world from which he questioned the mainstream narrative through scrutinizing the symbols that helped perpetuate it. These include the national flag and the coat of arms. He started questioning their circulation in the public domain. The body of work in the ARAK Collection comes from this series.

TRANSMEDIA STORYTELLING

In Phetogo's body of work in the ARAK Collection are a lot of interesting visible features derived from different media and reference points. There are what appear like direct geographical references in the form of contours depicting undulating surfaces on maps. The same can also be read as graphs on meteorological maps based on the shadings of colour between the spacings. The depicted landscapes also read like volcanic constructions characterised by sedimentary layers accumulating over ages of near eruptions. Some of the portrayals give an impression of distance, with layers of mountains building over a distance from the viewer's standpoint. In that case, they provide what art writer Thuli Gamedze has described as "infinite-potential surfaces," whose effect is to muddy the very idea of 'the beginning.'[10] Indeed, some of the paintings could be read as the cross-sectional views of the landscapes showing the mountains and their roots, and the water table too.

Whatever one's reading of the work is, I certainly see direct references to the Matsieng site, having been there in person. *The Foot and the Mountain* (2020)'s lower half appears like a bird's eye view of the site with the rocky surface painted in grey and interrupted by pools of water. The way the pools have been carefully placed suggests a complete paw. The upper half of it seems like the cross section of a mountain with the layered sediments presented in different colour shadings against a monochromatic green backdrop. The Matsieng reference also seems to apply to *Lowe (Male Hill Female Hill 2)* (2020) with the pool of water representing the pool out of which the mythical figure and the animals are said to have emerged from. With that reading, I am then tempted to say the multiple markings on the surface seem like cracks on the rocks, and yet they also take the form of boundaries for a subdivided land mass.

[10]Guns and rain. 2021. Thebe Phetogo- Ko Ga Lowe.

“The distance away from home gave Phetogo time to reflect and to question the notion of culture as fixed or unchanging in his country of birth… He started to critically look at how Botswana had negotiated and constructed their postcolonial identity, building on an ‘imaginary world’ centred on national myths.”

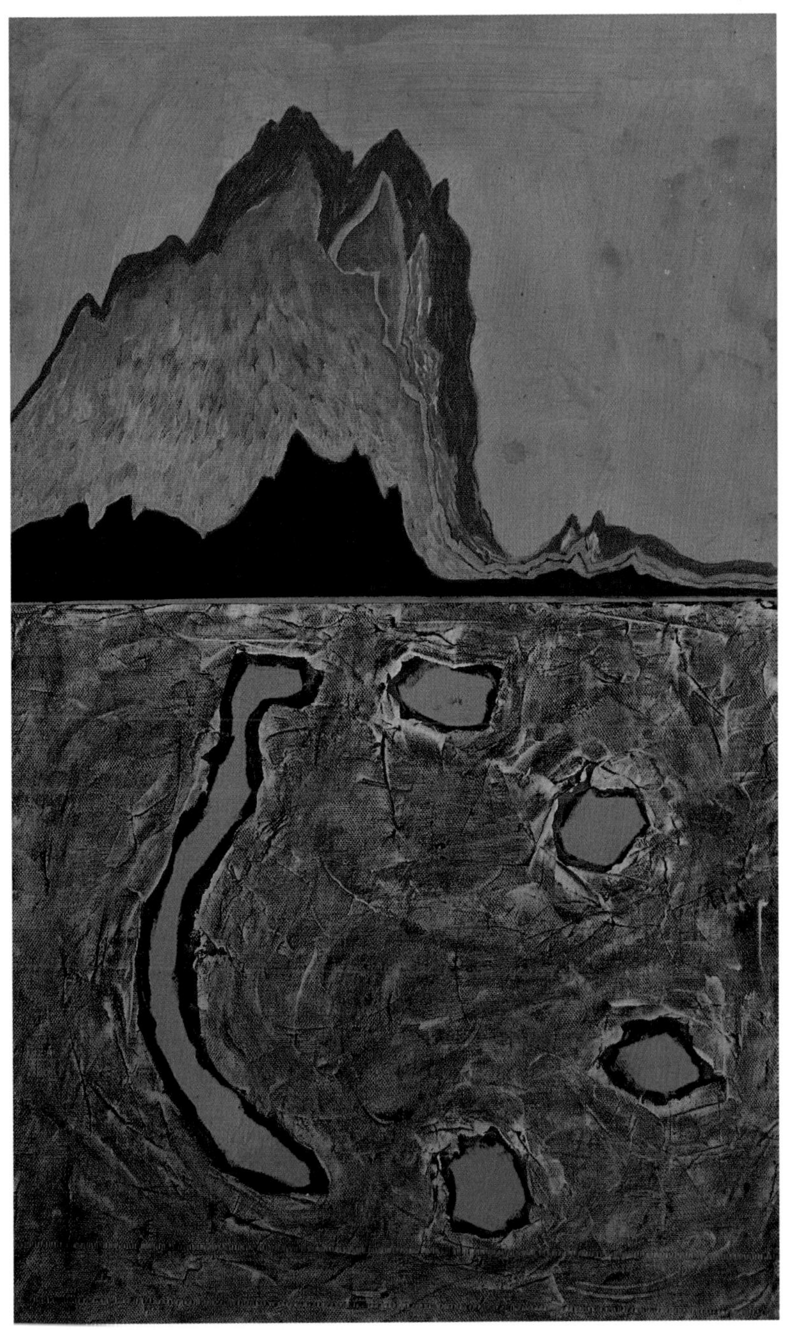

The foot and the mountain | Thebe Phetogo
2020 | 56cm x 34cm | Oil, acrylic and shoe polish on canvas

“There are what appear like direct geographical references in the form of contours depicting undulating surfaces on maps. The same can also be read as graphs on meteorological maps based on the shadings of colour between the spacings.”

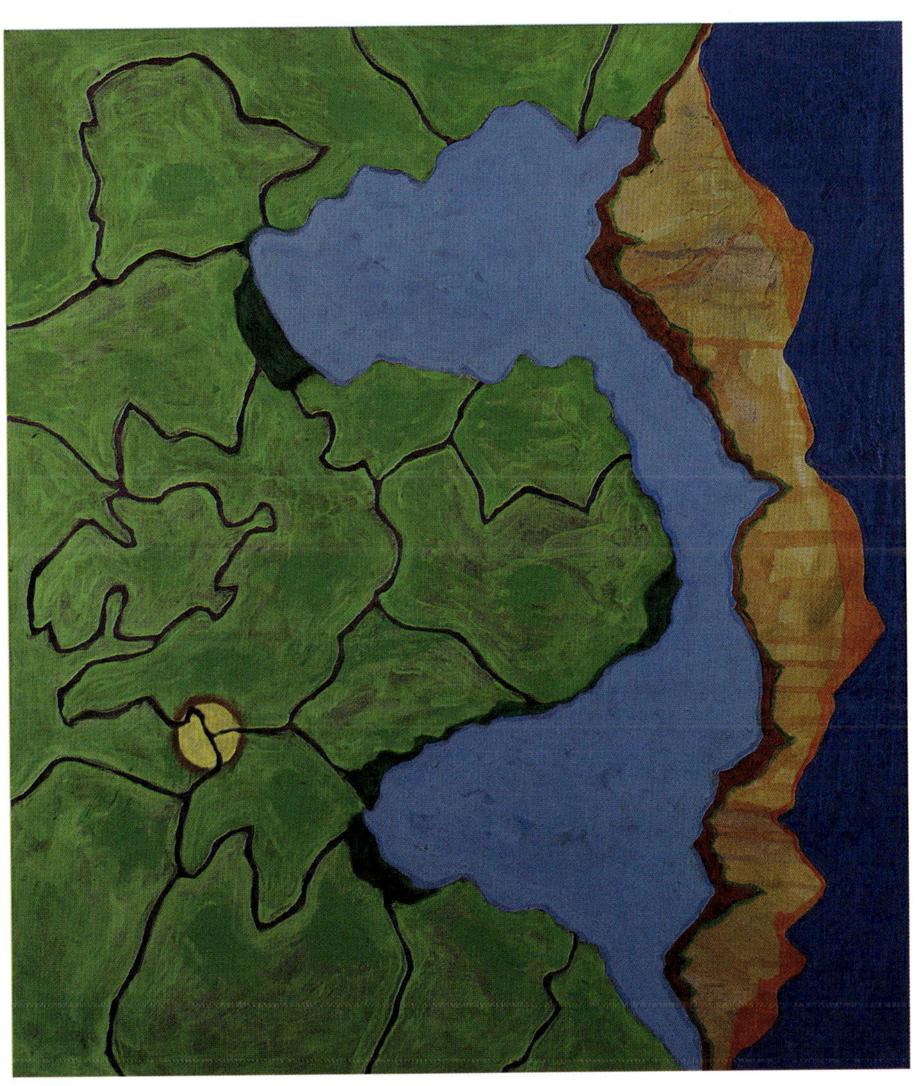

Lowe (Male hill female hill 2) | Thebe Phetogo
2020 | 44.5cm x 51.5cm | Oil on canvas

In Untitled (Lowe) (2021), Phetogo introduces the checkerboard backgrounds found in Photoshop transparency against a layered painting of multiple colours carefully arranged like in a graph. The checkerboard is a common pattern on stone monuments like Great Zimbabwe and many other smaller dry-stone-wall constructions in the region. *A blackbody as a Composite of Symbols* (2020) was part of a series of paintings in which he experimented with the idea of blackness, both as the absence and presence of colour, engaging how the Black body is perceived in the world. For the work, the artist experimented with shoe polish, enjoying the visibility the Black body has when presented against a colourful background.

Of the green and blue backdrops that are such a common feature of his paintings, Phetogo indicates that he sees it as a generative field or a theatre of dreams where he can create anything. It is like the television screen. In *The Simple Truth: The Monochrome in Modern Art*, Simon Morley quotes the philosopher Giles Deleuze as having declared the cinema screen "the frame of frames" as it allowed one to present both long shots and close-ups, as well as elements like relief and distance. The author goes on to state, "Instead, the cinema screen inaugurated the era of the blank rectangle as a receptor surface available for countless projections" (Morley 2020: 209). It is the same idea that Phetogo plays around with as he perceives the green screen as a space for performance and manipulation, as well as the ideal site to experiment with the borrowed ideas from retcons and worldbuilding.

Listening to Phetogo describing the green screen as the dream space of Botswana futures where he feels the freedom to create and imagine anything, I am easily tempted to consider the range of his references and his work as rooted in the domain of Afrofuturism. His portrayals are influenced by historical references of his nation, and of the realm of painting, he draws from speculative and scientific aspects, maps, and graphs employed in forecasting weather, empty panels of comic books, data visualization techniques, infographic and technical illustrations, and storytelling.

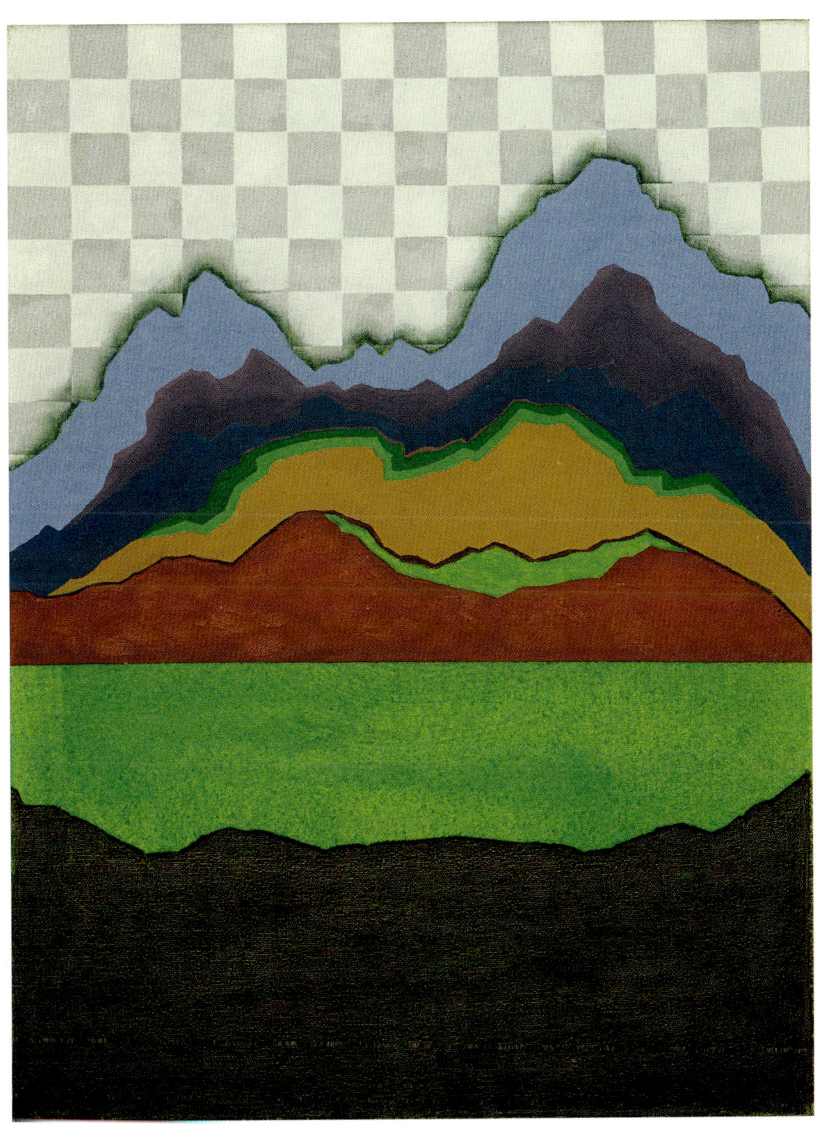

Lowe (Chess plate background with brown foreground) | Thebe Phetogo
2021 | 61cm x 46cm | Acrylic on canvas

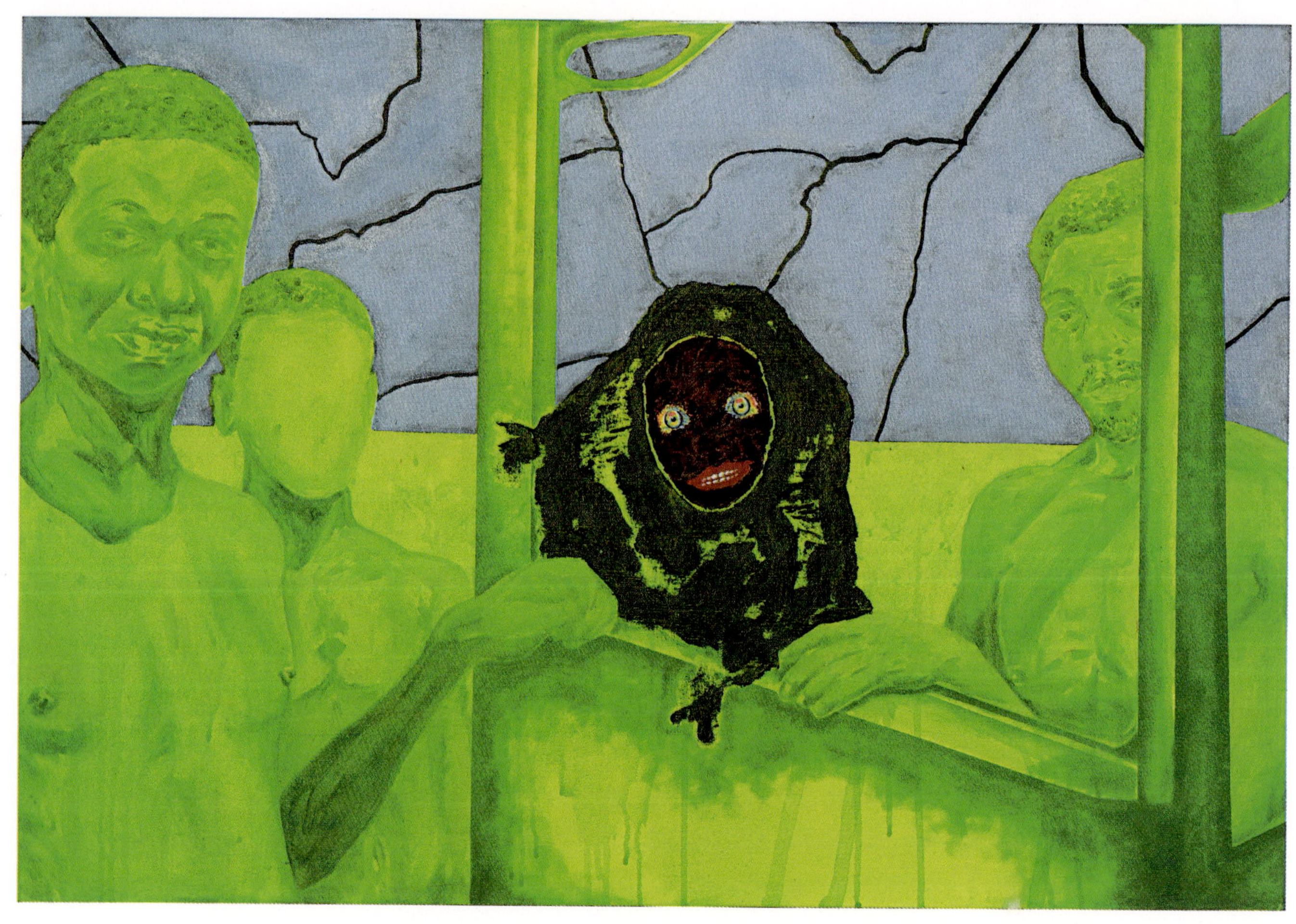

Watching as it Happens | Thebe Phetogo
2020 | 61cmx 91cm | Shoe polish, collage, oil and acrylic on canvas

OPEN ENDING

Phetogo's portrayals are not mere aesthetics. His experiment employs art to make Batswana reflect on the mainstream narrative of their nation's birth, and to imagine and consider other narratives. That is why it is crucial that there is no finality in his work. He is merely opening a discussion, equipping us with the tools to use following any direction, albeit with the potential to shake the dominant narrative. His effort is like Kalinosi Mutale's in that it also aims to draw attention to the narratives of the precolonial phase. Due to the lack of documentation and no visible culture of art writing, it is a bit hard to trace the history of painting in Botswana, especially dating back to the modern phase. However, he is among a group of young contemporary artists emerging out of Botswana and determined to shake the status quo. The majority of them are graduates of the University of Cape Town.

SECTION THREE

(VICTOR) MUTALE KALINOSI CHISHIMBA: BUILDING ON THE PAST

FROM THE MARGINS

My cousin, who was reading for a History and Development Studies degree programme at Midlands State University in Zimbabwe in the mid-2000s, once told me that one of his lecturers in introducing the topic of globalisation had this to say: "Globalisation entails that fruits are apples, oranges, grapefruits and peaches, not matamba, maroro and nhunguru." The lecturer went on to indicate that the concept had a certain language considered universal, while others like Shona and all other African languages are peripheralised. The last three are Shona names for different fruits, which I shall intentionally not translate into English. The lecturer argued that the three terms would never be used as acceptable universal names of the fruits. This example speaks to the dominance of colonial narratives and knowledge systems, which continue to overshadow African indigenous epistemologies. In this article on a selection of (Victor) Mutale Kalinosi Chishimba's abstractions, I attempt to reveal some of these ancient writing systems and argue why it is important for an artist to highlight such ancient forms of knowledge as he does. I was able to engage the artist on a fine afternoon at his home in the neighbourhood of Meanwood in Ndeke Village in Chokwe District, slightly more than 30 kilometres outside Lusaka, and near the Kenneth Kaunda International Airport, Zambia's main airfield.

SANKOFA DIALECTICS

In a book chapter titled "Recording, Communicating and Making Visible: A History of Writing and Systems of Graphic Symbolism in Africa," author Konrad Tuchscherer enlists and discusses some of Africa's ancient and modern writing systems. These include the alphabets of the Vai of Liberia, the Bassa in West Africa, and Adinkra of the Akan in Ghana. There was also the Nubian alphabet for the people of Sudan, the Kikakui syllabary that emerged in Sierra Leone, as well as Nsibidi, among the communities of Nigeria, and Gicandi in Kenya. As early as 1724, King Agaja of Dahomey is alleged to have experimented at inventing the Dahomey script. While the emergence of some of these writing systems are traceable to creative individuals who mostly claimed to have had a vision or revelation of some sort in their dreams, most developed organically and spread through diffusion as the communities migrated from one area to another. In Southern Africa, the rock paintings of the San groups, dating back 27,000 years ago, were left scattered all over the rock outcrops of the region. Moreover, the region is known for forms of writing, which appeared as decorative designs on clay ports and other ceramics, especially among the Bantu communities that arrived to disperse the San groups. These writing systems were important as they helped preserve and pass on local knowledge for generations.

In a recent article titled "Sankofa and the Afterlives of Makerere," Zimbabwean author Panashe Chigumadzi makes a call for Africa's liberation from what she refers to as the "tyranny of the Roman script wrought by late colonialism and the attendant myth that there are no prior traditions of written African literatures prior to European intrusion."

As the author unpacks, Sankofa is a form of Akan and Twi philosophy, which calls on us "to recover from the past what is good and bring it into the present." While Chigumadzi's premise is literature, I find the idea relevant to artistic practice as some of the ways of storytelling among African communities were quite graphic, characterised by symbols and other forms of representations, more than the letters of the alphabet. Chigumadzi is not alone in making such a call with many others before having emphasised the need for Africans to retrace their roots in different areas of study. A figure of note to have made such a call is Thabo Mbeki in the early years of his reign as the president of South Africa. In what he termed, the *African Renaissance,* Mbeki called for the revitalisation of Africa's cultural traditions and customs in their entirety. It is not a coincidence therefore that Mutale's work, referencing the ancient writings of the San groups, emerged a few years following Mbeki's call.

IN GOOD COMPANY

The ancient African writings offer insights into the past. As such, besides being a communication tool, they can also be considered a vital way of keeping records. According to Tuchscherer (2007: 45), "in most cases [these early] scripts were filled out with characters that were inspired by traditional graphic symbols that existed in the environment of the particular script inventors." This claim stands true if one is to consider the process followed by Mutale, with his inventions being influenced by the litany of San writings found on the granitic outcrops in his environment.

In inventing his own symbols or what he calls 'Kalidrawings' (derived from his name, Kalinosi), Mutale is not alone in thinking through ancient writings. He is in the company of other thinkers like the Zimbabwean writer Saki Mafundikwa, who authored *Afrikan Alphabets,* a project in which he engages the continent's long history of writing, and the late Togolese artist El Loko, whose desire to unite various philosophies in pursuit of an international or universal language (Krempel 2014) led him to inventing the *Cosmic Letters,* a project enshrined on the glass ceiling of the Zeitz MOCAA Museum, which also serves as the floor for the picturesque sixth floor of the institution.

As emphasised by Hassan and Oguibe (2001: 26), artists who engage in this form of practice are mostly "driven by the quest for self-representation and the negotiation of their identity." As such, their research into the past is also a way of confronting the legacy of colonialism imposed by the universal Roman script used in most parts of the world. Interventions of this nature tend to destabilise the narrow Western modernist canon by bringing in indigenous knowledge systems, which help prove that we had progressive 'civilisations' that were disrupted by the colonial enterprise.

CONCEPTUAL ARTIST IN ZAMBIA

Two scholars who have written extensively about the contemporary art scene in Zambia, Ruth Simbao (neé Kerkham) and Andrew Mulenga, have highlighted and discussed what it means to be a conceptual artist in Zambia. The two art historians agree that it is difficult to sustain conceptual and installation art in the country as it is perceived to be too foreign (European) or 'un-Zambian' by the local audience. This scenario mostly affects "Zambian artists who travel and study abroad" and is worsened by the fact that it is the "European and American donor community [which] pulls the strings in Zambia" that determines what "real Zambian art" ought to be (Kerkham 2007: 124). As such, it is not surprising that around 2004, Mutale and Anawana Haloba, as reviewed by Simbao, had an exhibition titled Konse Kubili (both sides of a coin), in which they tried to address both the local audience inclined to accepting works in media like prints, paintings, and sculpture, and an academically trained audience drawn to conceptual art and new media.

Regardless of the above-cited reasons that might dissuade some Zambian artists from engaging in conceptual art, Mulenga states that the genre has a fairly short history, traceable to the early 1990s, when Zambian artist Martin Phiri returned from studying in China and staged performances that shook the local art scene. Phiri is said to have made a series of hyper-realistic casts of his face, placed one of them in a casket, staging a funeral in which his wife and close relatives mourned his imaginary death. Over the years, artists who had international exposure like Lutanda Mwamba, David Chirwa, Victor Mutelekesha, Baba Jaken Chande, Mutale, and Haloba (Mulenga 2016) continued to engage in conceptual art.However, as Mulenga (2016: 67) argues, their practice "in Zambia has gone virtually undocumented [yet this is an art form which] finds breath when written or documented." Moreover, if it has been shunned by the foreign donor community patronising the local art scene, could it be the reason why Mutale, who seemed to have been more vested in conceptual art, seemed to have stopped making work and actively participating in shows in Zambia? Could it also be a case of the few existing galleries in Zambia not being well-equipped to sustain the art form? Although prominent local galleries like 37D appear to embrace conceptual art, they mostly lean towards showcasing figurative works. However, the situation on the ground is certainly changing as an institution like the Modzi Arts Gallery is seen at the FNB Art Joburg, showcasing conceptual art at times, and new players like the Lusaka Contemporary Art Centre have come into the fold.

INSPIRED BY ANCIENT SAN WRITINGS

Mutale encountered reproductions of the ancient San rock art paintings at the Livingstone Museum. According to Sam Challis, a researcher at the Wits University's Rock Art Research Institute, the people who left the paintings are the indigenous hunter-gatherer communities of Southern Africa, who are the first peoples of the region. Depending on countries in the region, they are either referred to by the terms San or Bushman. In Zambia, for example, Mutale kept referring to them as the latter, while in South Africa, the descendants of the communities mostly embrace the former. *Challis* (2022) indicates that both terms were initially quite derogatory and demeaning, "but now both have been reclaimed as identities to be worn with pride."

The pigment used for the paintings left by the first peoples of Southern Africa were mostly done using charcoal, soot, and carbon black, with a mixture of fat. They were mostly done for religious and spiritual purposes, especially for scenes of healing the sick. The communities had a special relationship with the depicted animals. The paintings were mostly done in caves and on rock outcrops in most parts of the region. The ones at Silozwane in the Matopo National Park in Zimbabwe and the one in the Drakensberg Mountains in South Africa are known to be the most elaborate within the region. Silozwane is a living site considered sacred by people from the Matabeleland region of Zimbabwe, who still go to worship at the shrine. Interestingly, the communities which perform rituals at the site today are the descendants of the Bantu farming communities responsible for displacing the first peoples of the region.

The San communities have been pushed to dry and difficult-to-inhabit areas like the Namib Desert and the Central Kalahari Game Reserve in Botswana. Based on positionality, Mutale is an outsider of the community. However, his work highlights the histories of these marginalised community, which stresses the role artists can play in reviving narratives that ought to be occupying centre stage in a bid to foster a culture of inclusive development in the region.

CYNICISM OR THE REALITY OF AFRICA

Ranging from what appears like a little bunny painted in black to an imperfect circle in black to a yellow footprint to a pair of red speakers and two balls of thread presented in blue, and so on, the non-conventional symbols or abstractions depicted by Mutale lack any recognisable content leaving the body of work open to the viewer's interpretation. Colour tends to represent something in art, yet in this case, it does not seem to do so, hence, we do away with the clichés of association, especially when one considers the titles ascribed to the works like *Abase* and *Abattoir.* Could there be a relationship between the depicted symbols and the message the artist is trying to put across?

What quickly jumps out for me are the titles of the works in the ARAK Collection. The artist's descriptive titles are all loaded concepts in the form of nouns. Through its highly suggestive titles, the work takes the viewer into another realm or mental zone, not presented to them on a silver platter. As a result, the viewer ends up making associations they would have never imagined. When I asked the artist about his titles, he indicated that they are the concept conveying the message in the work. Therefore, they are not just some random words.

In the works titled *Boy Crocodile* (2004) and *Girl Crocodile* (2004), Mutale indicates that when he made the two artworks, he was concerned about the destabilisation of external forces on the continent of Africa. From Joseph Kony's Lord's Resistance Army in the countryside of Uganda, the civil wars in Angola, to the Democratic Republic of Congo, at that time, the use of child soldiers was rampant. An indoctrinated child soldier becomes a killing machine, who can even wipe away their own relatives or parents. Therefore, the two pieces somehow freeze time, drawing our focus to what was taking place at the time they were made. The child soldiers lose their innocence and have no empathy whatsoever. Therefore, the work highlights the existence of the dehumanised child.

Also related to the degrading situation referred to above are works like *Abase* (2006) and *Abattoir* (2006). The latter refers to the way innocent people are massacred in times of conflict and compares it to the way cattle are slaughtered on industrial farms. Through *A-Bomb* (2006), the artist asks himself rhetorical questions like Why the need to manufacture a bomb? *It serves and saves who? And what would the world be like without the wars that go on every now and then?* When I ask him about the title *About Face* (2006), which appears like a musical note, the artist starts talking about a difficult moment he experienced while living in Europe, where he felt he was not seen as human as everyone around him because of his skin colour and different face. His explanation reminded me of a story I heard from a friend who witnessed a member of the San community being told to "go back to the bush" by fellow passengers on a public taxi on the streets of Gaborone. They saw him as an outsider still belonging to an inferior civilisation. Could being on the receiving end of the tense, condescending European gaze possibly be the reason for Mutale's interest in the stories of the marginalised communities of the San, or he was just fascinated by their sophisticated forms of writing?

Although the work engages a difficult moment in the trajectory of Africa, and therefore carries a heavy and pessimistic message, what I admire about the artist is his ability to navigate and portray what was happening without having to reproduce images of pain. Although quite different in form and genre, the work reminds me of Chilean artist Alfredo Jaar and the way he worked on *The Rwanda Project* without having to reinforce problematic images of the genocide.

When it comes to the materials he used in the process of producing the work, Mutale indicates that his use of pastel was inspired by the simple way the San people used plant pigments to write. "I did simple drawings in simple form so that when I am not there the viewer can tell the story by relating the drawing to the title. These are symbols I have not seen before. I was just applying my brain to create. Random images would pop up when I came up with the concept," says the artist.

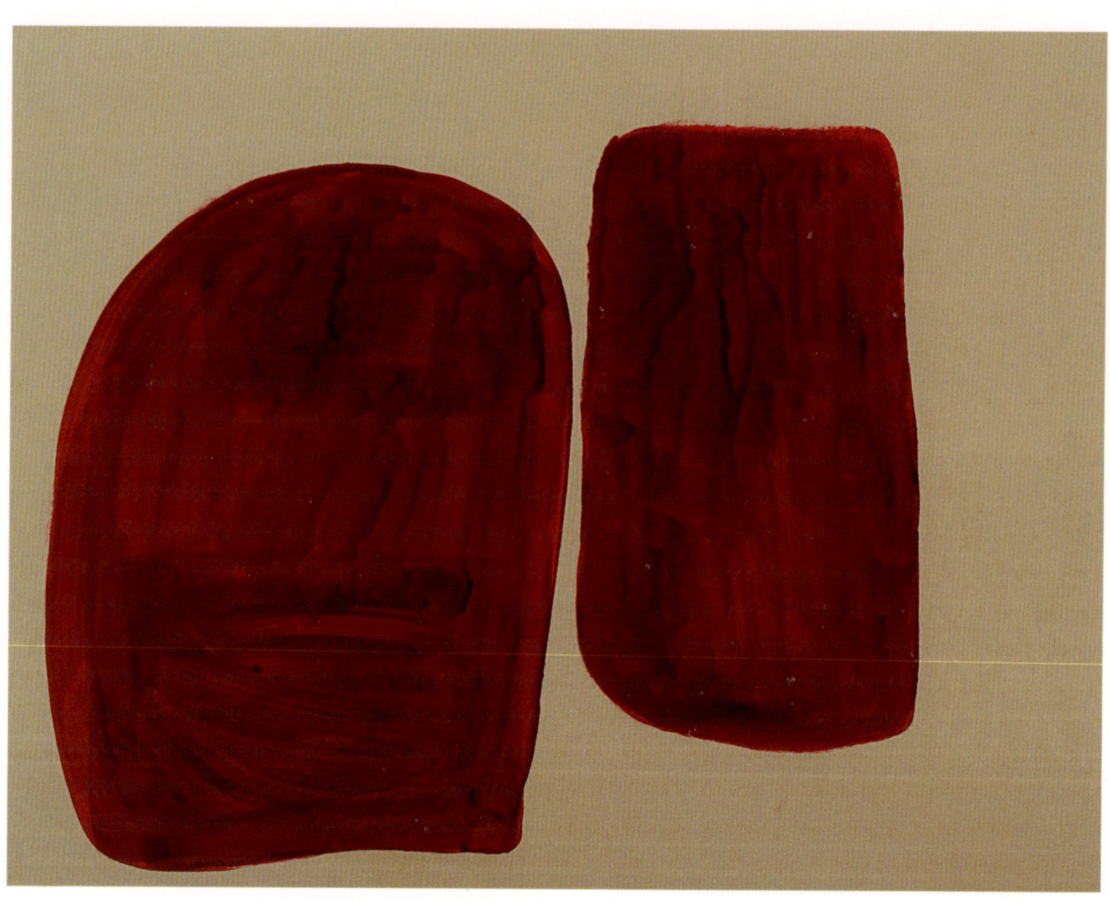

Boy crocodile | (Victor) Mutale Kalinosi Chishimba
2004 | 50cm x 65cm | Ink on cardboard

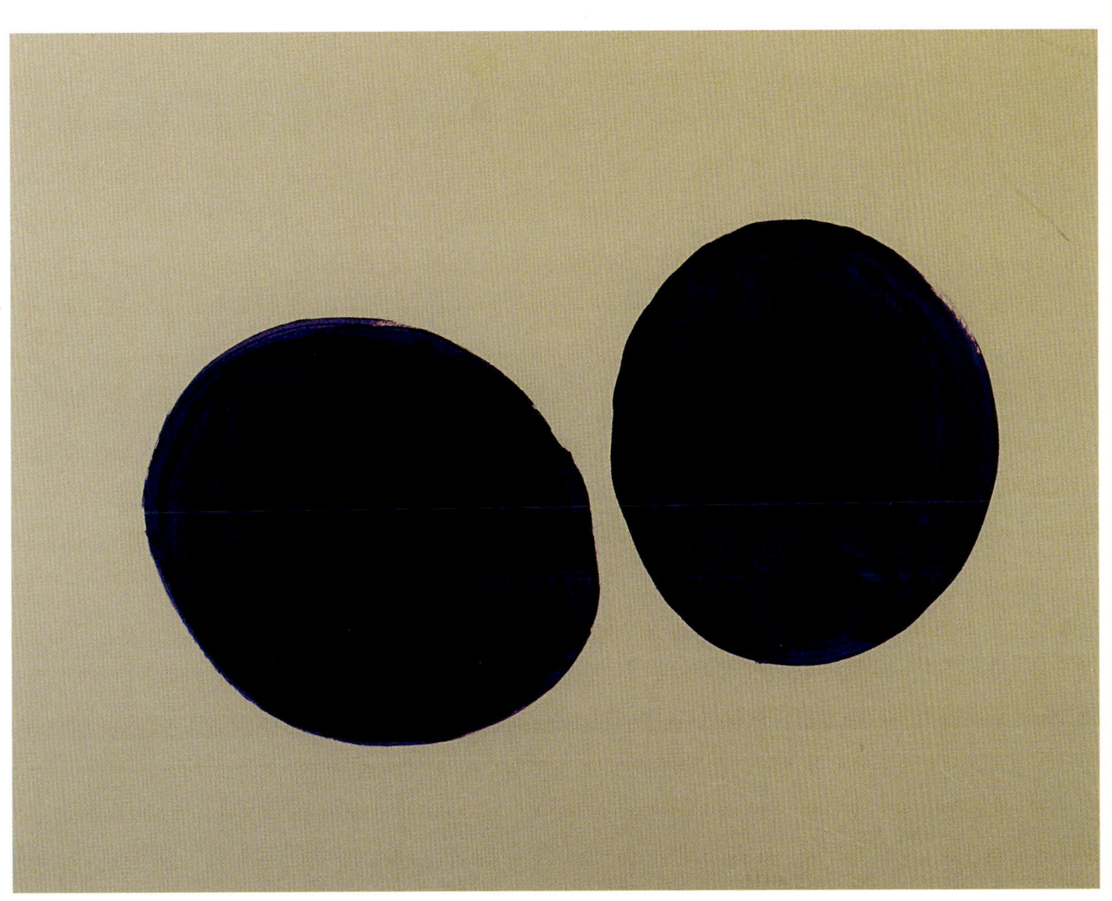

Girl crocodile | (Victor) Mutale Kalinosi Chishimba
2004 | 50cm x 65cm | Ink on cardboard

"The ancient African writings offer insights into the past. As such, besides being a communication tool, they can also be considered a vital way of keeping records."

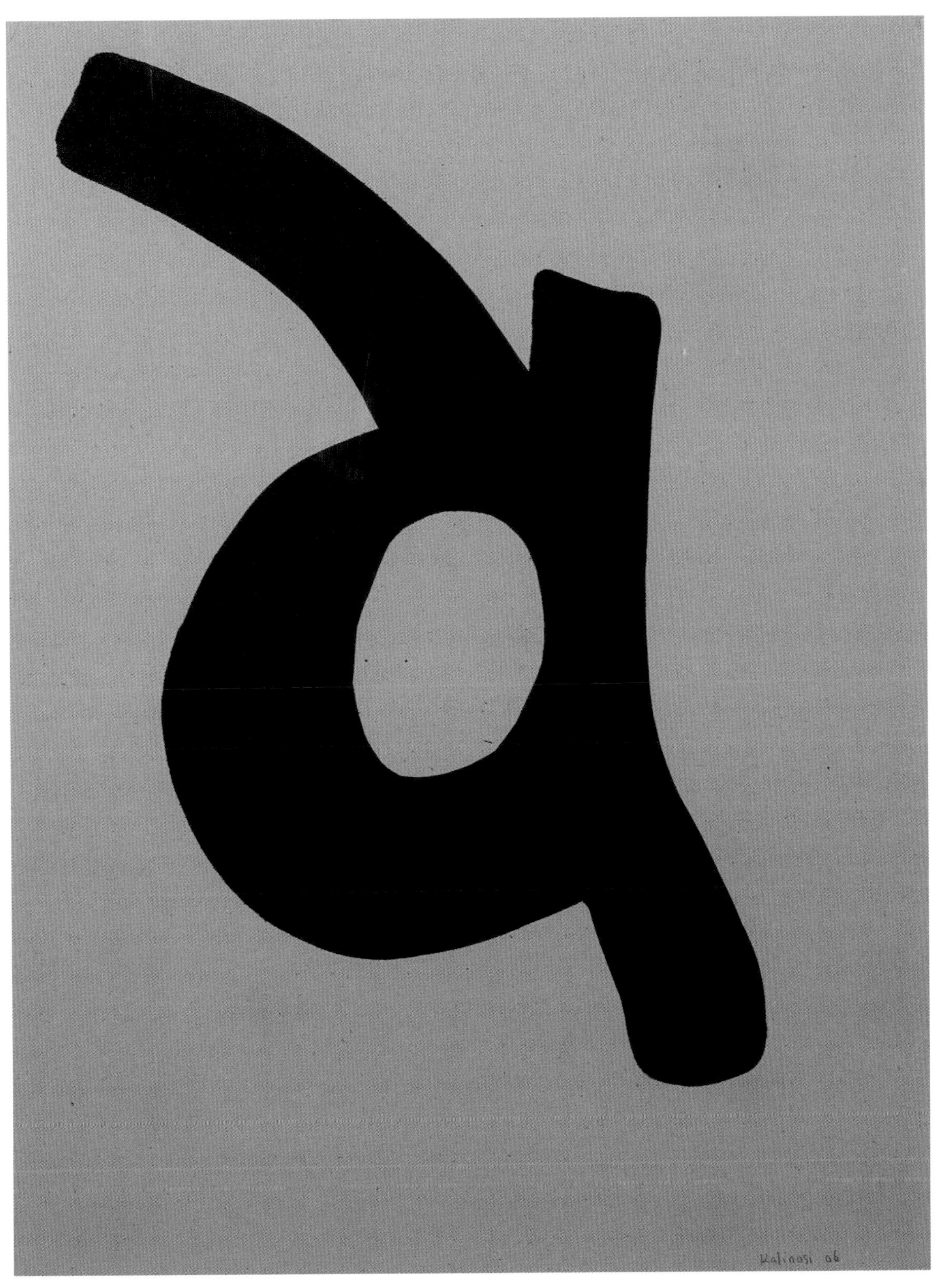

Abattoir | (Victor) Mutale Kalinosi Chishimba
2006 | 71cm x 53 cm | Ink on cardboard

“The distance away from home gave Phetogo time to reflect and to question the notion of culture as fixed or unchanging in his country of birth… He started to critically look at how Botswana had negotiated and constructed their postcolonial identity, building on an ‘imaginary world’ centred on national myths.”

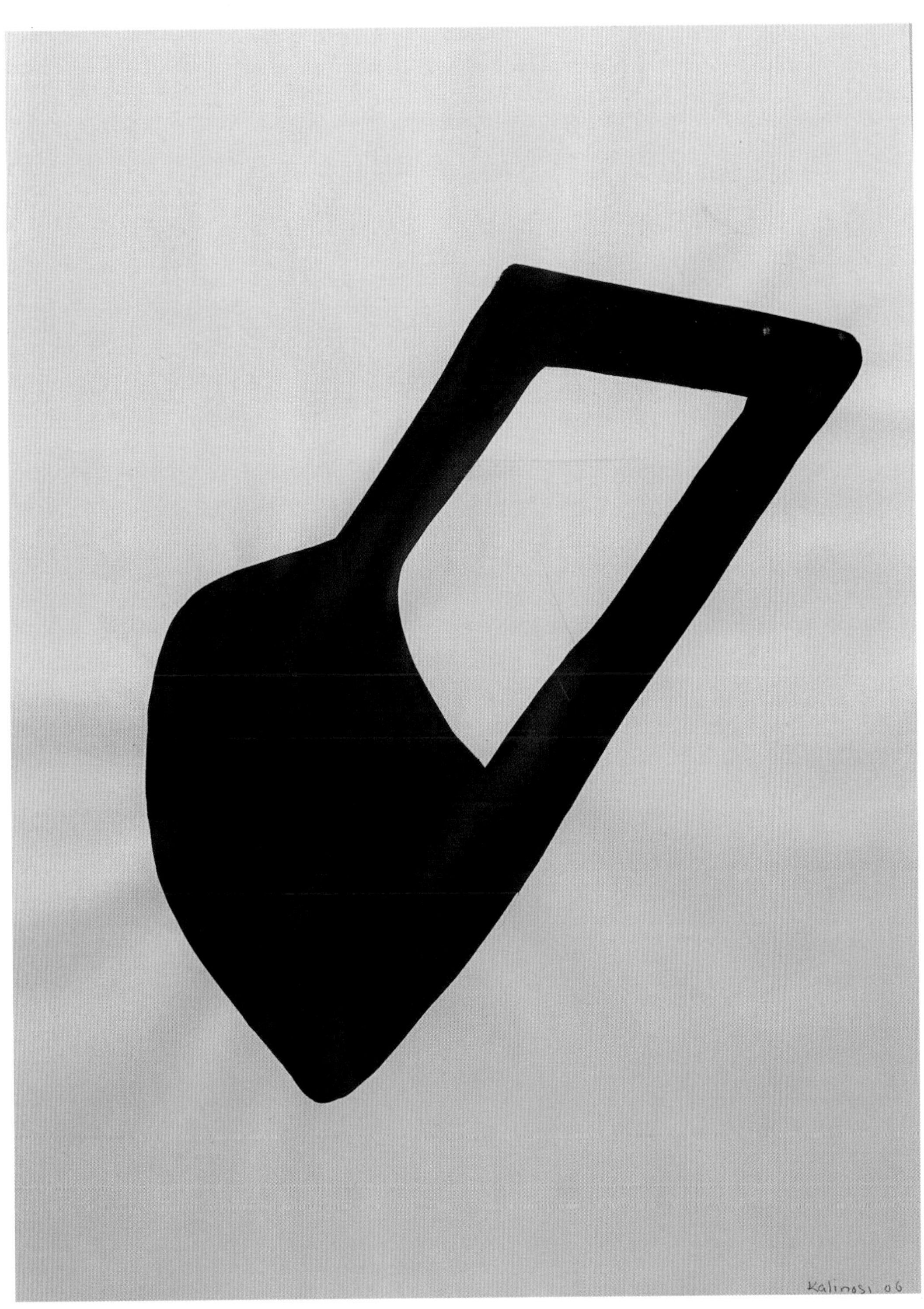

About Face | (Victor) Mutale Kalinosi Chishimba
2006 | 61.5cm x 47 cm | Ink on canvas

"I did simple drawings in simple form so that when I am not there the viewer can tell the story by relating the drawing to the title. These are symbols I have not seen before. I was just applying my brain to create. Random images would pop up when I came up with the concept."

— (Victor) Mutale Kalinosi Chishimba

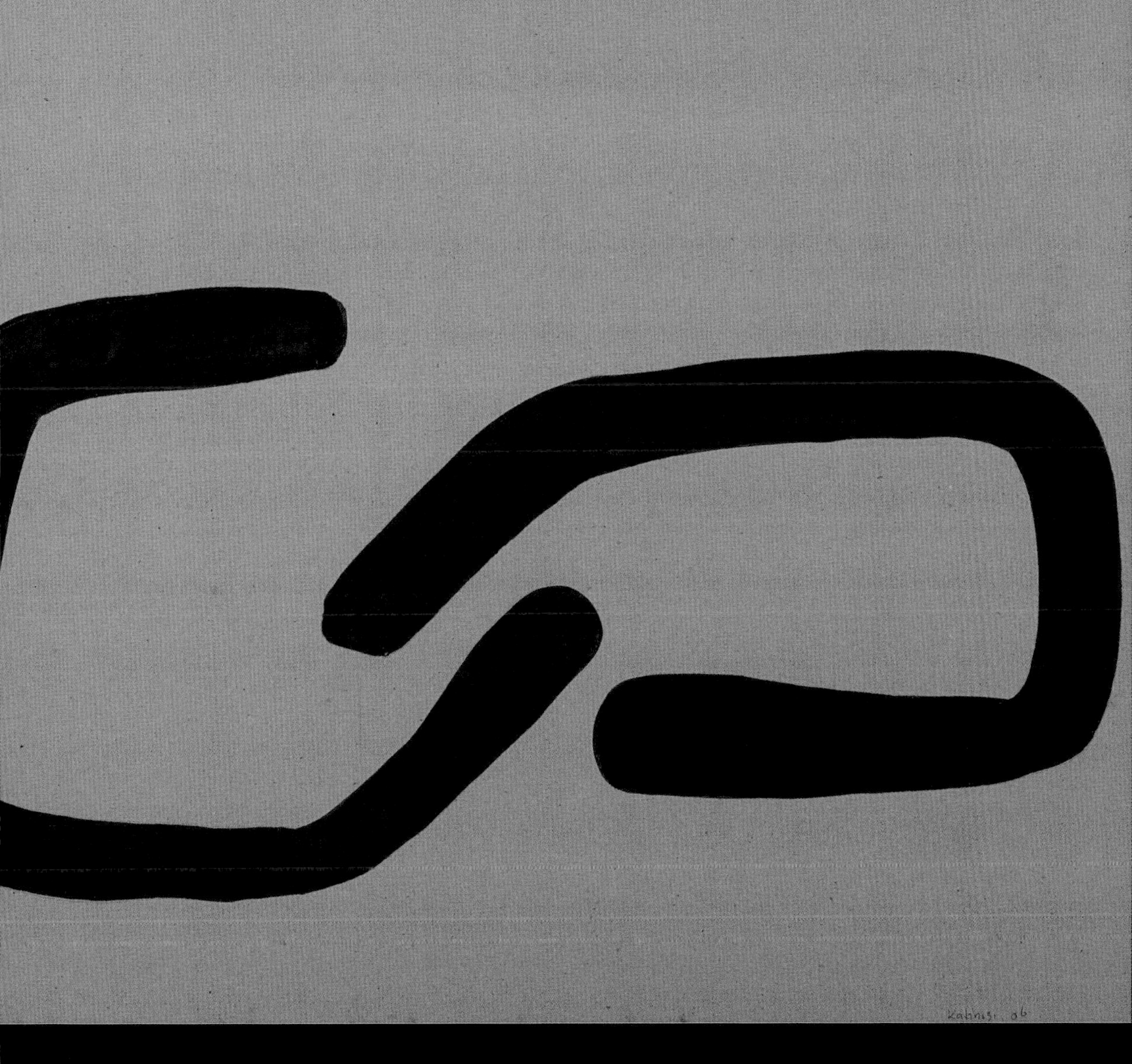

Entoil | (Victor) Mutale Kalinosi Chishimba
2006 | 53.5cm x 70.7cm | Ink on cardboard

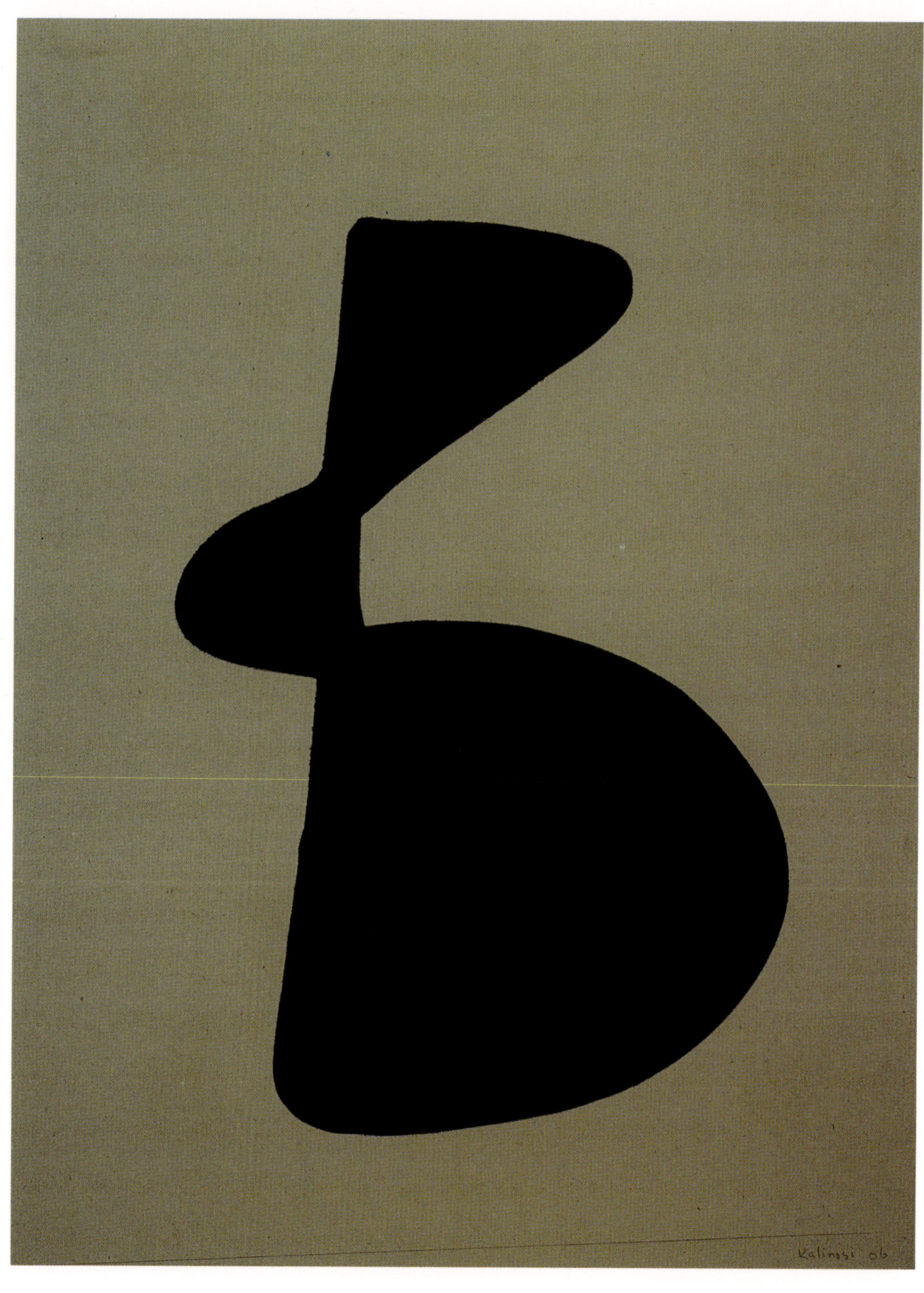

Abase | (Victor) Mutale Kalinosi Chishimba
2006 | 71cm x 54cm | Ink on cardboard

A NECESSARY INTERVENTION

Southern Africa's first peoples or indigenous communities were the several hunter-gatherer San communities who were displaced by the arrival of the more sedentary Bantu farming communities. Interestingly, not a single government in the region has embraced San culture to an extent of including their language among the official languages spoken in their countries. Only South Africa has at least included their motif on the nation's coat of arms. The descendants of San communities have been pushed to the peripheral inhospitable environments, as in the case of Botswana, where they occupy the Central Kalahari Game Reserve. These are some of the mistakes made in the postcolonial African states. Mutale's initiative to reference the San writing systems may not necessarily save the ignored and dying cultures of the region, but it is critical in that it attempts to preserve the script at a popular level. It also draws our attention to a form of writing, which existed in precolonial Africa. While Mutale uses his invented symbols to address a problematic subject, he at least does so without having to reproduce figurations of the dehumanised subject, thereby making a clever intervention.

SECTION FOUR

NELLY GUAMBE: REFLECTIONS AS CATHARSIS

THE MOTORBIKES AND THE CHOPELA

I arrived in Chimoio at sunset on Saturday, the 5th of August, en route to Maputo. I disembarked from an *overloaded Kombi* (public minibus) at the town's central marketplace. Most of my fellow passengers had been Mozambican nationals deported from Zimbabwe. After a few minutes, I found myself surrounded by several bikers, all shouting and scrambling to ferry me to the place where I had booked my accommodation. Our first problem was there was a total breakdown in communication between me and them. I was trying to convey my message in English. It would even have been better if I had spoken to them in Shona as Chimoio is closest to Zimbabwe and many people in the Manica Province of Mozambique speak my language well. It feels like Manica is the extension of Zimbabwe's Manicaland Province, which stretches along the eastern border of the country, covering Mutare and the Forbes border post, through which I had entered Mozambique. The second immediate problem was I had a backpack and a small suitcase, which made it difficult for me to sit on a motorbike while holding them.

It was in the ensuing chaos that a policeman came, grabbed my passport, and asked me to follow him. I felt safe and did not hesitate to follow. Suddenly, there were about four other guys insisting on assisting me, with one of them speaking in Shona as the police officer had said he could neither speak nor understand a word of both Shona and English. Others even wanted to carry my bags for me, yet I could easily manage them. After a minute of walking, I found myself flanked by two police officers brandishing AK47s demanding to see my COVID-19 vaccination certificate. This was about a year after the World Health Organisation had declared that people could travel around the world freely again. Just to show how odd the officer's demands were, I had been to four other countries in the region, and none of them required me to produce the certificate. When I managed to retrieve an e-certificate, which had been emailed to me by the Department of Health in South Africa after I received my doses, the officer found me at fault for not printing it. He wanted to see a hard copy. Sensing that there was no other way I would get out of the situation, I had no choice but to pay him the money he was demanding. I was also worried that the situation might get worse, and I would end up losing the DSLR camera and the laptop I was carrying in the bag. Luckily, I had some Mozambican meticais on me and as such, they did not have to search through my bags.

Suddenly, the area I grew up respecting as a place where the Rhodesian forces massacred Zimbabwean civilians during the country's liberation struggle—as immortalised and memorialised in song and political rhetoric—became menacing for me. On the same night, I made sure I booked myself on the earliest bus to Maputo the next morning. In all the countries I had been to on this research journey, I got off at city marketplaces and easily found my way out via the local taxis. The drivers were super friendly. Contrary to that, the many riders on the Chimoio market caused a lot of chaos and the language barrier complicated everything. When I arrived in Maputo, I did not encounter the same problem, but I also found out that there were plenty of motorbikes on the road. However, what seemed to cause chaos on the capital's roads were the local tuk tuks known as chopela. The little scooters are designed to carry one or two passengers without much luggage.

Riding a motorcycle on Southern Africa's roads is quite unsafe, regardless of which country one is in. I remember soon after I arrived in South Africa over a decade ago, two of my friends were hit by cars in separate accidents at road intersections, with one of them severely injured. The problem seems to be that no driver respects the riders, sometimes even acting like they do not see them. If this happens in a country like South Africa with its state-of-the-art roads, then one can imagine what happens in its neighbours with terrible road networks, save for Namibia.

after I arrived in South Africa over a decade ago, two of my friends were hit by cars in separate accidents at road intersections, with one of them severely injured. The problem seems to be that no driver respects the riders, sometimes even acting like they do not see them. If this happens in a country like South Africa with its state-of-the-art roads, then one can imagine what happens in its neighbours with terrible road networks, save for Namibia.

I started by narrating this story, which helps provide context for the state in which artist Nelly Guambe was in when she made the body of work in the *Silent Reflections* series, about ten of which are in the ARAK Collection. She was confined to her apartment having just been released from the hospital, slowly recovering after suffering a broken vertebra. Apparently, Guambe had been hit by a car while riding on her motorbike on Avenida 24 de Julho in the heart of Maputo. A few months prior to the incident, she had acquired a bike imported from Denmark, which she was using while working for a non-governmental organisation. The bike made travel in and around the city convenient. Without necessarily revealing who was at fault, she tells me she was hit by a female driver.

RESTORATIVE PRACTICE

The first time I set my eyes on Nelly Guambe's works in the *Silent Reflections* series, I thought they were prints. Knowing that some artists approach printmaking from a painterly approach and viewers can even see visible rough brushstrokes on them, I could see editions of reproductions. Despite the range of variations in quantity and colour, they looked similar as prints do and are all a specific size. They carry magnificent detail, yet the faces seem not to express much emotion. A closer look at them reveals that some of the faces have lesser and larger features, while the rest have more and smaller features within the frame. It is a technique the artist employs, which gives the impression of them having been zoomed in and out, or cropped in the same manner a photographer frames the subject. Yet these are pastel drawings made directly onto the paper. In most parts, they are so dense that one is tempted to call them paintings. The rough strokes on them are obvious. The Cubist-inspired distortions of their foreheads, noses, and mouths are also visible. Some of the faces are brighter, while others are quite dark. Perhaps their hues depended on how the artist was feeling at the time she drew and painted them, with the brighter ones being from the days she was feeling better, optimistic perhaps, and had sweet memories, while the darker ones might have been done on days when she felt stuck in a deep hole. One or two are even too abstract to read as faces.

The works in the *Silent Reflections* series are all made on A5 paper. At the time she made the works, Nelly had broken her vertebrae, and she spent time lying on the bed as she had to be in a flat position all the time. Yet her compulsion to create stayed alive. In the artist's words:

At the time I was slowly gaining strength, recovering some movement, and becoming self-reliant, faces were the only feature I could do. Faces appeared a lot in my memory. There were faces where I was. I could do nothing else, but I enjoyed seeing colour.

Scientists talk of a rare condition called prosopometamorphopsia, which is some form of visual disorder characterised by altered readings of faces. To a person with that condition, faces appear distorted and strangely disfigured as seen through exaggerated eyes and teeth. In most cases, the contorted faces appear with displaced features. The body of work created by Nelly at the times seems to exhibit all these characteristics. However, the alternative to that is she could have simply been influenced by the Cubist painters like Pablo Picasso and Georges Braque, who were notorious for disfiguring and deconstructing faces.

Whatever it was that motivated her to present the faces in the manner she did, this body of work documents a moment when the artist was vulnerable. "At the time I had so many difficult personal reflections. I was asking myself if I could handle pain. If I was prepared to handle pain," she explains. Yet when painting kicked in, it helped her kick out the stress. She stopped worrying as she got invested and absorbed in every picture and artwork she worked on. The process helped occupy her brain and mind as she slowly found her way back into the world of creating. Thus, painting became a coping mechanism or a way to stay alive and a form of catharsis.

In her usual practice, Nelly Guambe turns her gaze on women she encounters in her everyday life and work, highlighting the issues and circumstances they face. Interestingly, she documents them in ways that do not objectify them, but manages to provoke the viewer's thoughts, leaving them with many unaddressed questions. The ARAK Collection has six of such works, three of which I will highlight here. The first one to draw my attention is *Victoria* (2019), a portrait of a stylishly dressed woman with a decorated grey and pink dress that matches the elaborate headgear. The dark monochromatic background propels the work forward and makes sure the viewer gets to engage the figure with no distractions coming from behind the work. The artist's ability to vary the dark hues of the woman's skin tone and that of the background is quite impressive. The varying hues are also a prominent feature of the work titled *Retrato de Uma Mulher* (2017) with the artist managing to make the figure's hair and clothing stand out to reveal the face. As highlighted above, the artist manages to place the figure against a grey monochrome that does not disturb the work at all. However, the yellow abstracted background in *Memorias* (2017) somewhat takes away certain elements from the main figure. It is hard to tell whether the woman in the work is also wearing a yellow jacket that blends into the background, or the shoulders are missing from the portrait. The yellow background also somehow overlaps onto the hair. Otherwise, the different shades of grey that mark the dress, the hair, and the face are applied well, and the features really stand out.

I am interested in reading the faces of the women in Guambe's work as masks of a kind. A mask is an object that conceals the face. I am persuaded to apply this metaphorical reading of the work due to the way the women in the work either return the gaze onto the viewer, or by their refusal to do so. While in *Memorias* the figure refuses to make eye contact, the women in the other two stare back at us. The stare in *Victoria* is even more assertive, if not intimidating. It is not easy to tell a person's story from the gaze alone, but the random faces one encounters on the streets have a lot to say. Among them are souls who have been rejectedand are trying to reclaim their identity, people who have been divorced and are yearning for love, those who have triumphed over inner battles and are celebrating. There are mixed emotions out there, and yet Guambe's figures are usually serious and stern looking. They seem to have been through a lot.

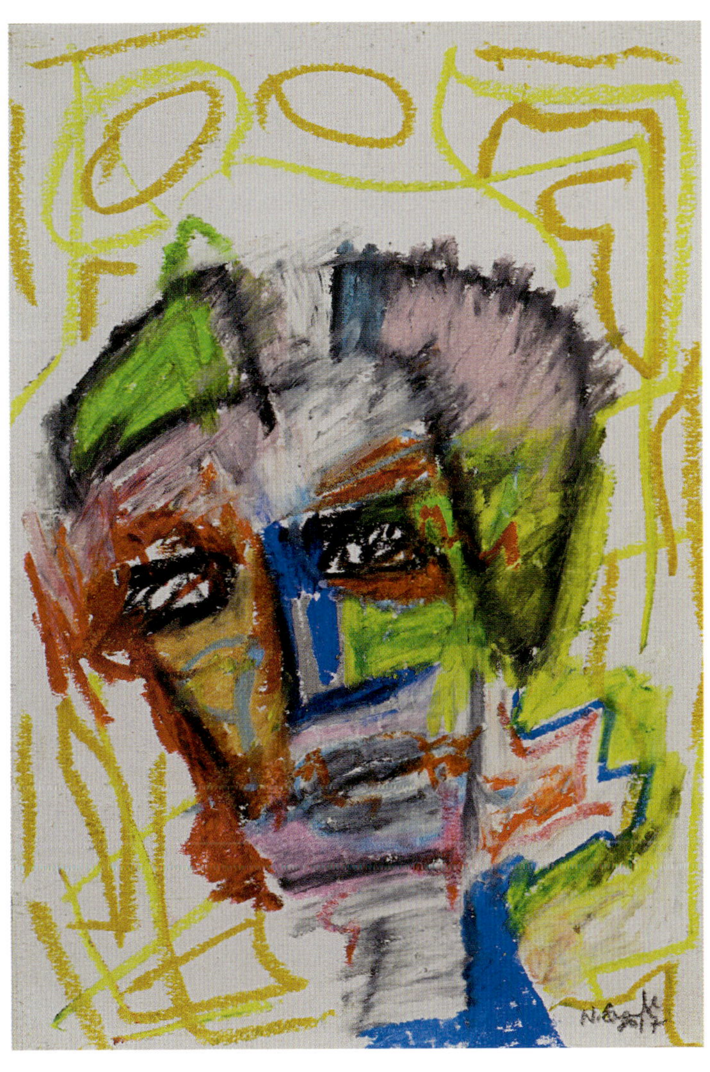

Silent Reflections | Nelly Guambe
2017 | 21cm x 14.8cm | Pastel on paper

“Nelly Guambe turns her gaze on women she encounters in her everyday life and work, highlighting the issues and circumstances they face.”

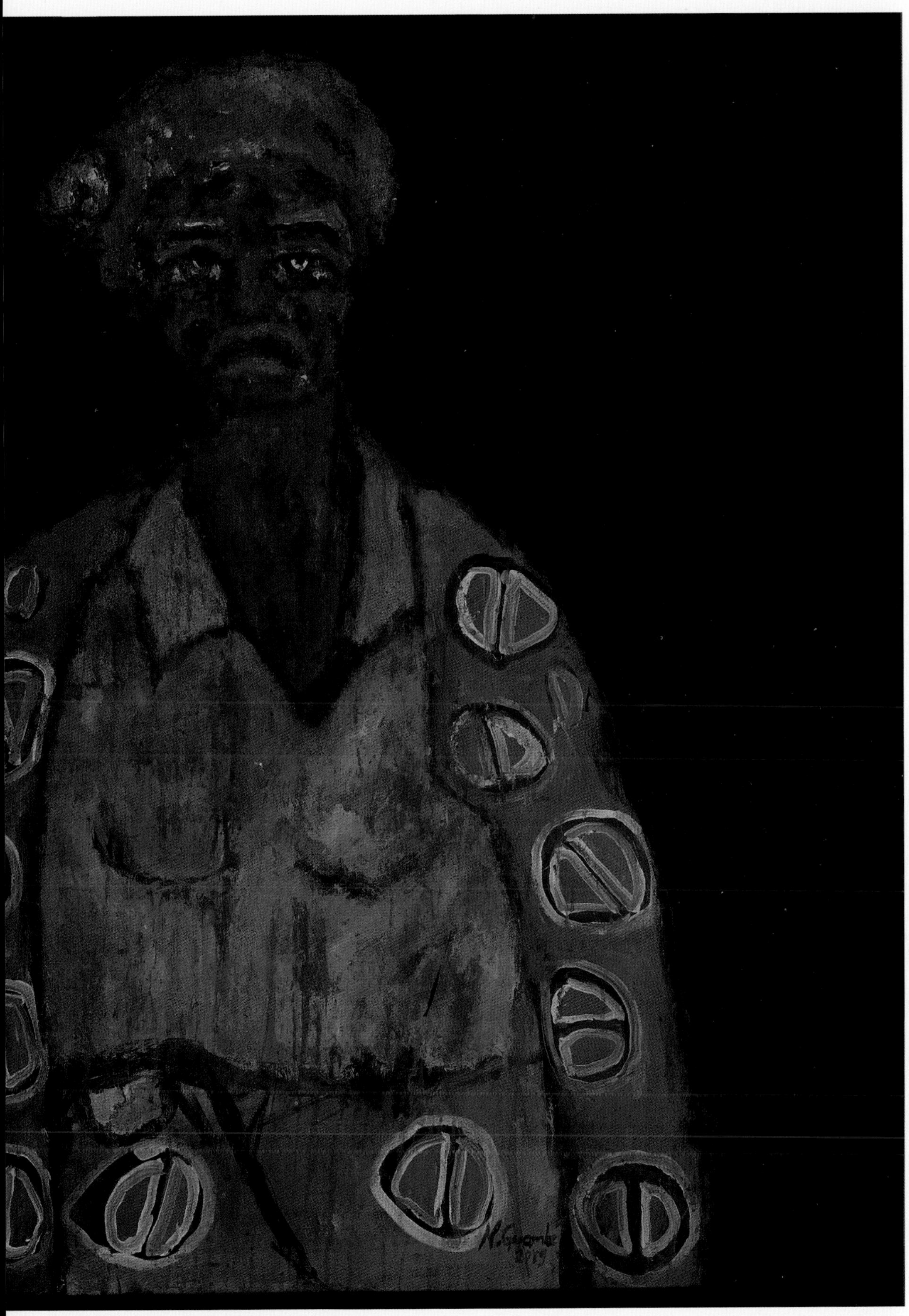

Victoria | Nelly Guambe
2019 | 100cm x 100cm | Acrylic on canvas

“I am interested in reading the faces of the women in Guambe’s work as masks of a kind… I am persuaded to apply this metaphorical reading of the work due to the way the women in the work either return the gaze onto the viewer, or by their refusal to do so.”

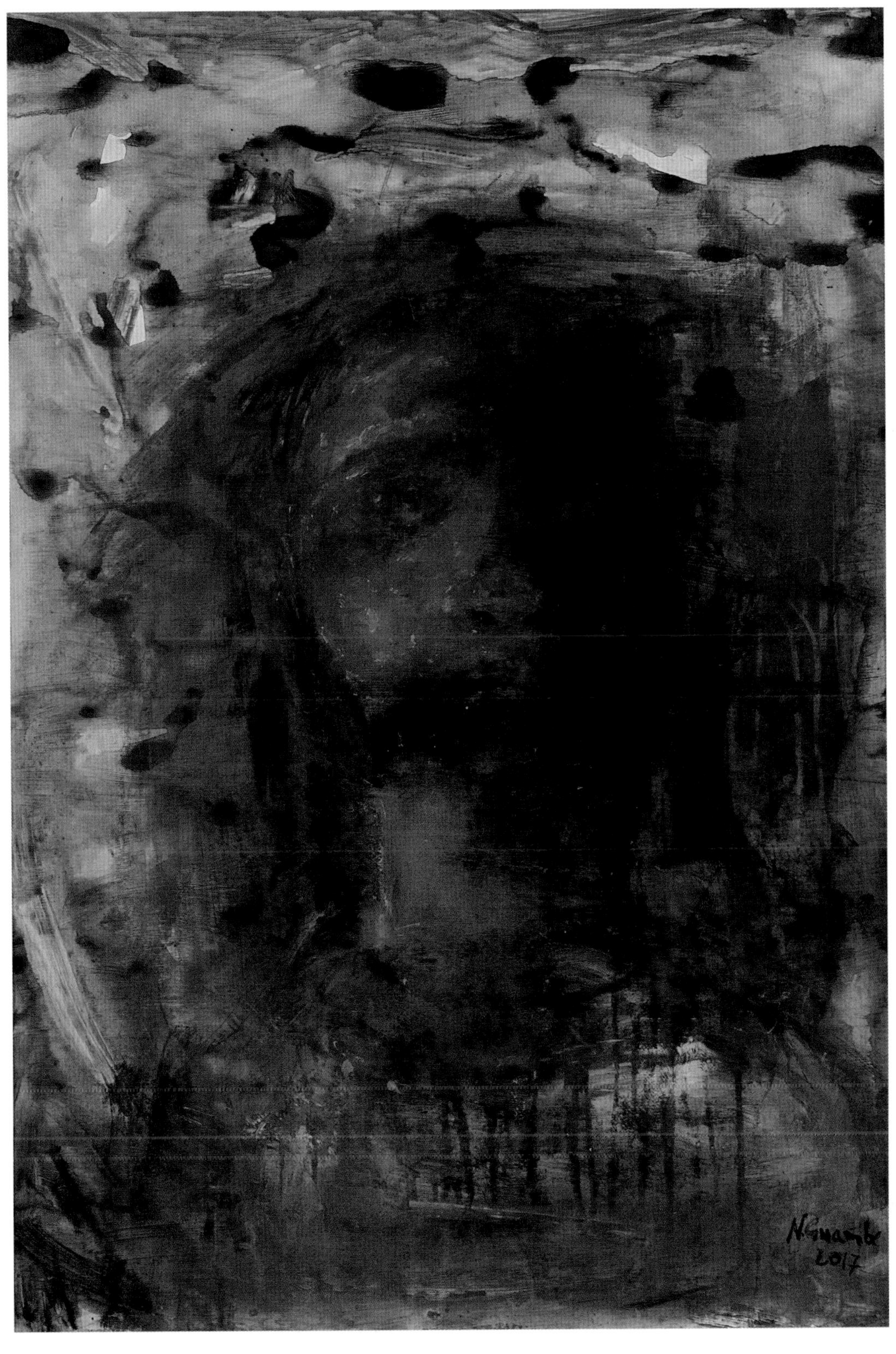

Tempo Estranho | Nelly Guambe
2017 | 86cm x 60cm | Acrylic on paper

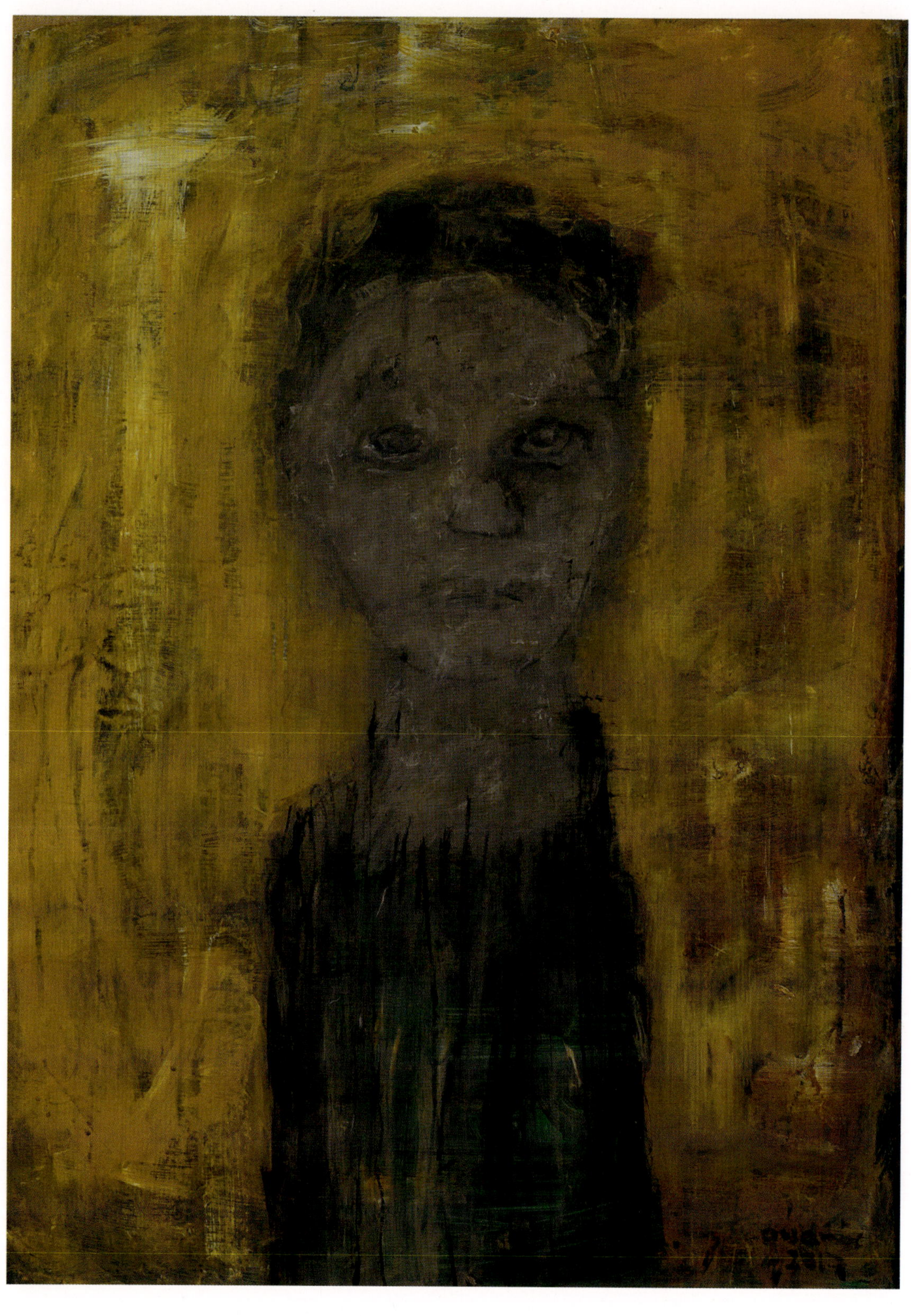

Memórias [memories] | Nelly Guambe
2017 | 82cm x 60cm | Acrylic on paper

CONCLUSION

Nelly Guambe's *Silent Reflections* series is a body of work which is quite distinct from her usual practice and her past work. She made the work at a time when she was quite vulnerable, and yet the process of generating the work helped her recover from injuries sustained in a road accident. In this essay, I also discussed three of her works from the past, which fall under the category of what I would characterise as her usual practice documenting the quotidian lives of individual women the artist encounters in her country. Mozambique is a country with a long tradition of painting and sculpting dating back to the colonial days, with The Centro Social & Cultural Do Nucleo De Arte playing a central role in the development of art in the country. However, although there is literature on painters like Malangatana Ngwenya and Bertina Lopes, there has not been any extensive documentation of art over the years. As such, it is hard to gauge the contemporary practices of painters like Nelly and Nelsa Guambe against that of artists from days gone by.

SECTION FIVE

LUTANDA ZEMBA LUZAMBA: TRANSNATIONAL NARRATIVES

SITUATING THE ARTIST'S PRACTICE

I recently worked as a research assistant for the Curatorial Department at the Zeitz Museum of Contemporary African Art (MOCAA), situated at the V&A Waterfront in Cape Town, South Africa. In the year I worked at the institution, I assisted the curatorial team with research for the *When We See Us* exhibition. The ground-breaking show focuses on Black figuration, highlighting how Black peoples in different "Black geographies" across the world have portrayed, presented, and celebrated themselves in the past century. Among the artists whose works were included in the show is Lutanda Zemba Luzamba. While researching for that show, I learned that the artist, who comes from Lubumbashi in the Democratic Republic of Congo (DRC), is part of a long lineage of Congolese artists who do figurative painting. Among them are celebrated elderly contemporary artists like Cheri Samba and Cheri Cherin, both of whom were included in the show at Africa's biggest museum of contemporary art. Although their subject matter and painting styles slightly differ, their practices help cement the fact that the DRC is a country with a great tradition of figurative painting, with some of it even hyper-realistic.

After traveling to neighbouring countries in Southern Africa, I came back to meet Luzamba, who is based in Cape Town in South Africa, where he works with Ebony Curated, a gallery with space in the central business district of Africa's most beautiful city. When I arrived at his home, which doubles as his studio, I could see stacked piles of his work, and the books and magazine publications he has been included in. On the wall along the passage, I saw the artist's own small, diverse collection of works from artists such as Khaya Sineilwe, David Khoulibally, Maurice Mbikayi, Sam Nhlengetwa, Ricky Baloyi, Steve Bandoma, and Malcolm Dare, among others. One or two works stood on their own as they were still drying. On the easel was a large, stretched canvas dissected by equally spaced, thin, horizontal and vertical lines. The lines are his first step when painting, yet there will be no visible trace of them on the final work.

A body of works painted on the traditional chitenge fabric captured my eye. Although popularly known as chitenge in Zambia and the DRC, they are general printed fabrics used for making women's dresses and headwraps commonly referred to as 'African attire.' In most cases, women always carry them in their handbags as it is considered respectful to wrap a chitenge around one's waist and on top of their dresses, especially at cultural ceremonies, funerals, and other functions. The colourful, wax-printed fabric, originally from Indonesia, is also referred to as 'kitenge' or 'Ankara' in Ghana and parts of West Africa.

In Zimbabwe, it is known as 'Zambia,' since the first supplies were coming from their neighbour north of the Zambezi. The artist indicated that he had painted on that fabric when he focused on the theme of migration. Such work and its transcultural references speak to the transnational nature of the work Luzamba makes and the narratives he transmits to the world. His story is also always embedded in his practice with the artist having lived and attended school in neighbouring Zambia, before going back to DRC and then moving to settle in South Africa.

Early in the year, I had encountered the artist's work as he had a solo show at Ebony Curated. Titled *Totem*, the exhibition employed the concept of the fables or folklore used to entertain and pass on wisdom from one generation to the next in African societies. Although the tradition is slowly dying because of urbanisation and exposure to technology and social media, it is still practiced in rural areas, where kids gather around a hearth (iziko) to listen to their grandmothers' stories. The text for the show was provided by Khanyisile Mawhayi, a curatorial assistant at the Zeitz MOCAA. In the short essay, Mawhayi stated:

Although there are conceptual and stylistic evolutions with this body of work, fashion and dress code remain key parts of Luzamba's practice. Like the sapeurs who inspired his previous works, the characters are impeccably dressed, with accessories such as gold watches, spectacles and hats that give us clues as to their age and who they may be in society.

Sese Seko's banning of Western suits between 1972 and 1990. The long-time Congolese leader preferred the Abacost, a suit designed like Mao Tse Tung's and coming in either short or long sleeves. It was also quite popular with socialist oriented African leaders like Julius Nyerere and Kenneth Kaunda. As a response to Mobutu's edict, the La Sape movement became synonymous with defiance and freedom. As an artist engaged in Black figuration, Luzamba considers it his duty to portray Africans in the best possible manner to counter the stereotypes about Africa, in which it tends to be seen as the continent of poverty, war, and suffering.

Luzamba's figures are depicted against different backgrounds ranging from the flowery chitenge one referred to above, to the block-coloured ones and to the rather simple abstracted monochromatic ones. In some of his paintings, the act of stripping the background of any material is quite intentional. It is the artist's way of removing noise or taking away any above, to the block-coloured ones and to the rather simple abstracted monochromatic ones. In some of his paintings, the act of stripping the background of any material is quite intentional. It is the artist's way of removing noise or taking away any distractions that may stand in the way of the viewer fully engaging with the figures. The removal of the contextual backdrop makes the figure stand out.

COMMUNICATING IN SYMBOLS AND GESTURES

While some of the subjects of Luzamba's work are recognisable individuals who are mostly from the family and public figures, the artist sometimes composes them from his head. Even when he portrays people we know, the work is usually deeply conceptual, and we can make sense of it if we can read and understand certain symbols and gestures that carry the artist's message to the world. What follows is a discussion of selected works in the ARAK Collection.

In New Beginning I (2018) is a figure of a man holding a white mask, which we are not sure whether he is taking it off or in the process of wearing it. The immaculately dressed man has a navy-blue outer coat with gold buttons. Underneath the coat is a black jacket inside that can also be seen on the arms, which are longer. Inside the jacket is what appears to be a coral jersey. The most telling feature are the man's deep forehead wrinkles. The figure is set against a monochromatic background, which makes it stand out without any backdrop noises. As the artist enunciates, the work signifies the change one goes through in the process of growing up or moving to a new environment. One has to come out of the old cocoon in the same manner a snake sheds its skin. The change can be about physical movement from one place to another, or spiritual. "The work comes from a series of three or four pieces and among them is one that highlighted about the lightening of skin which is something common among young African ladies [yearning for acceptance in societies which seem to appreciate lighter complexion]. It is a process that just does not happen automatically. There is the mental side of it where an individual starts by questioning their appearance," says the artist. The individual then goes on to decide. The work is also quite personal for the artist, who moved to Zambia for education and went back to the DRC before embarking on the journey to South Africa. He had to adapt to different situations on his journey.

What appears like a highly confident man is portrayed in *Le Combattant /Freedom is Not Free* (2017). He is dressed in a striped suit, with a pocket square that matches the white collar of his red and white striped shirt. With his two fingers raised in the air signalling the victory sign, what is surprising is the same hand is dangling a pair of handcuffs. He looks quite stylish with his fedora hat and a grey waistcoat. The red tie he is wearing is popular with political leaders.

The green monochromatic backdrop pushes the figure closer to the viewer. According to the artist, the dangling handcuffs signify a lack of total independence. The work is a direct reference to politicians, who campaign for positions of authority promising the masses all sorts of revolutionary transformations, yet they are not able to change the political system each time they get into the office. One wonders whether they grab all the attention and the votes to only go into the office where they end up enriching themselves instead of shaking the system. It is a case of individuals who fail to walk the talk. With the artist coming from Francophone Africa, he could also have been thinking of France's relationship with its former colonies, where the Central Bank of France still has direct control of their economies. It is that relationship that the leaders of the recent coups d'état takeovers in Mali, Niger, Burkina Faso, and Gabon are trying to break away from. "Only when the handcuffs are taken away, then you can talk of freedom. Under colonialism both hands were tied, now it is just one, meaning the freedom is partial," explains Luzamba.

New beginning | Lutanda Zemba Luzamba
2018 | 76cm x 61cm | Oil on canvas

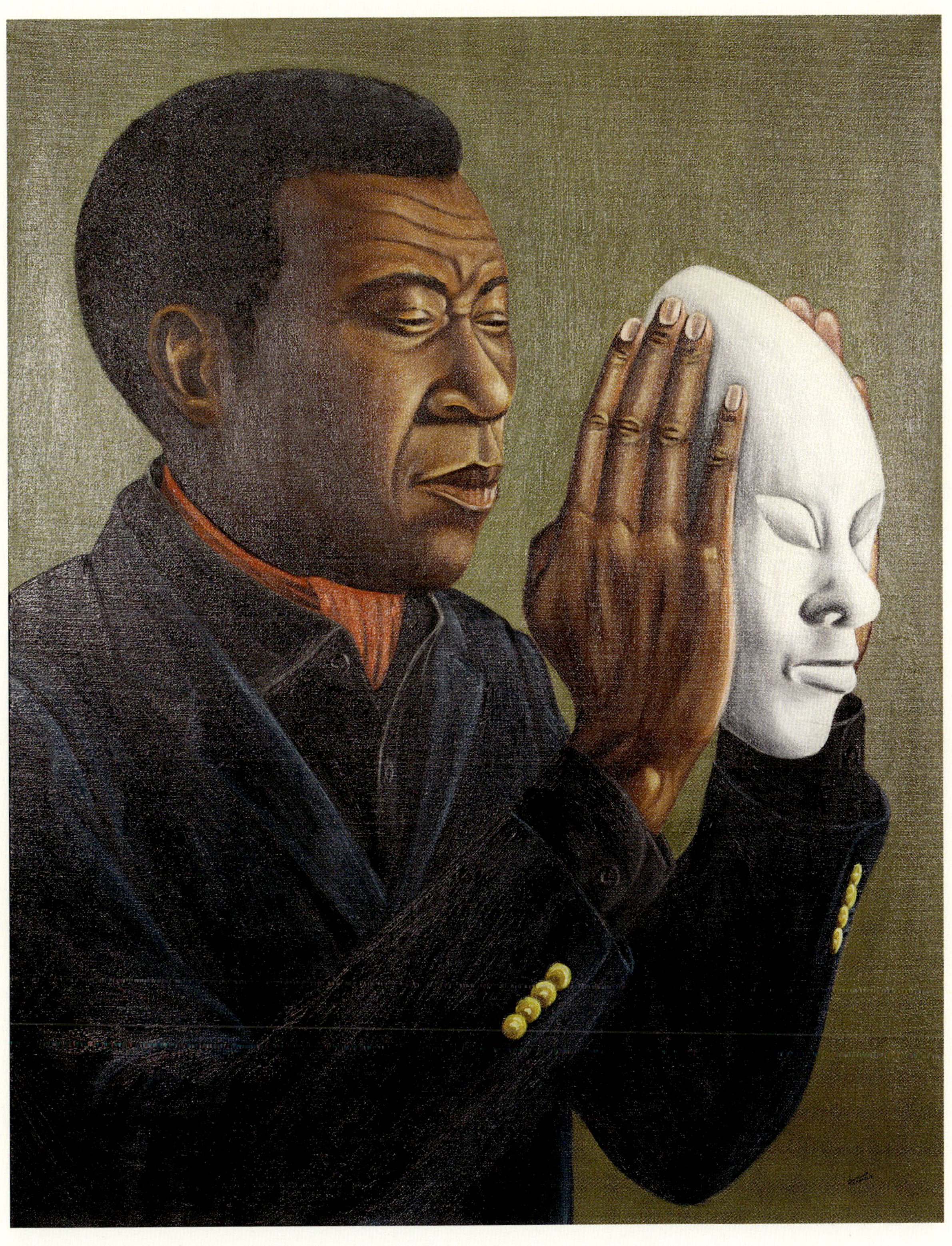

"As an artist engaged in Black figuration, Luzamba considers it his duty to portray Africans in the best possible manner to counter the stereotypes about Africa, in which it tends to be seen as the continent of poverty, war, and suffering."

Le Combattant /Freedom Is Not Free | Lutanda Zemba Luzamba
2017 | 103cm x 79cm | Patel on paper

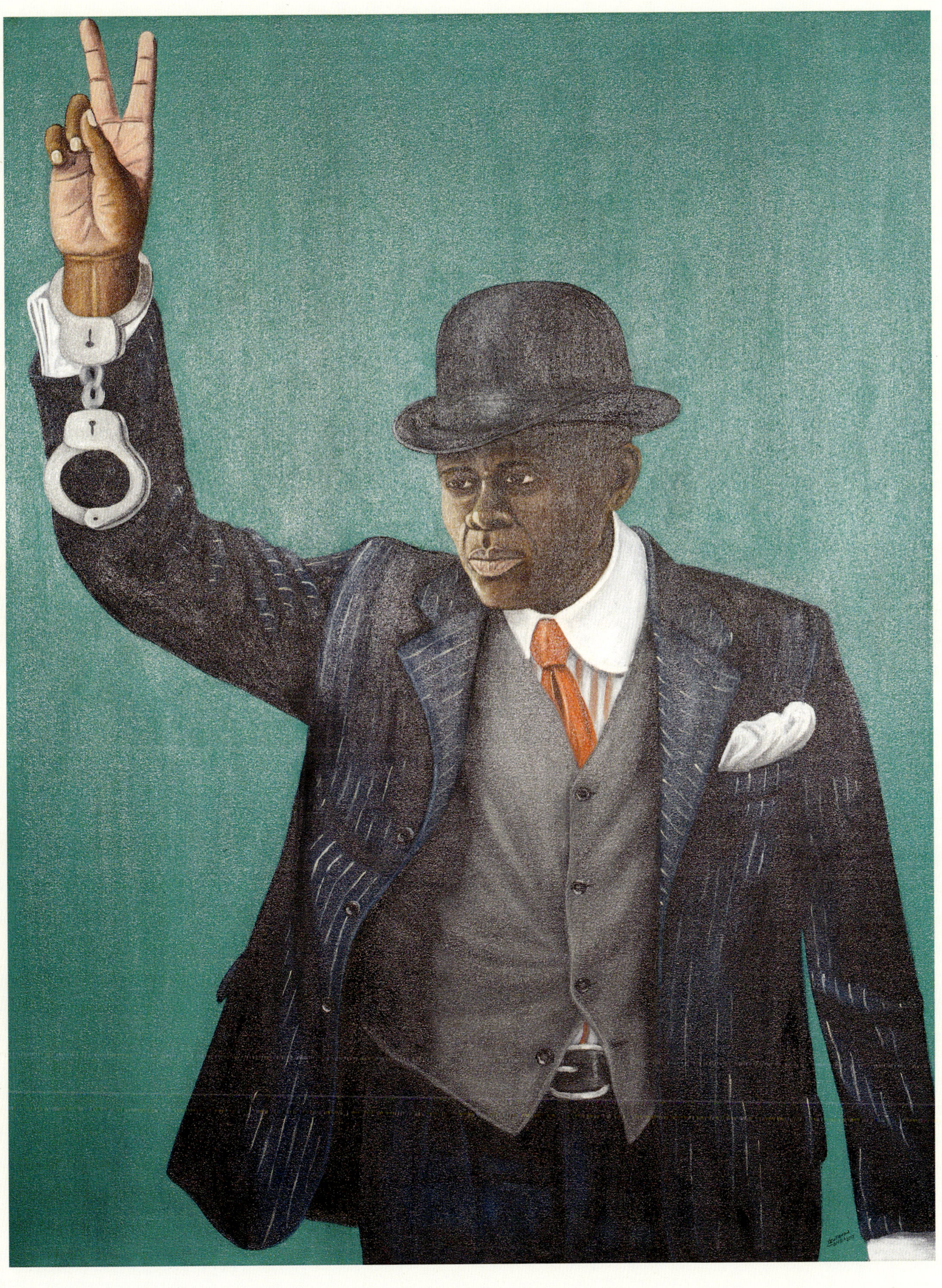

One of the artworks in which Luzamba presents a known figure is *Strategist* (2019). The painting is done on board, with the figure painted over a collaged background of newsprints. Sometimes the background reveals in the main image as is seen on the figure's arms. Just like in the La Sape tradition, the subject in the painting—Robert Mugabe, the former president of Zimbabwe—is dressed well in a Western styled suit. Before the early 2000s, when he was sanctioned from traveling to the United Kingdom, legend had it that he would travel to Harrods in London to buy his suits. A combination of his impeccable dressing, his eloquence in the Queen's language, and his repressive rule earned him Zimbabwean writer Percy Zvomuya's description, the nomenclature 'Afro-Victorian dictator.' With the word "Beyond" inscribed behind the figure, the collaged background speaks to the message the artist is conveying. According to Luzamba, the painting was done from a still image of one of Mugabe's interviews on Al Jazeera. The artist manages to replicate Mugabe's hand gestures and the confidence seen through his relaxed sitting posture. "The man used his hands a lot. I say strategist because he was a smart guy. I look at him in a positive way. He was someone who could defend himself properly in interviews and debates," says Luzamba. The way Mugabe is loved and praised by the rest of Africa is something that surprises Zimbabweans who suffered under his rule, especially the people of Matabeleland and the Midlands, who suffered the Gukurahundi genocide in the 1980s. In the man who failed to unite the country's two main ethnic groups, fellow Africans found a Pan-Africanist who could unite the continent. To Luzamba, Mugabe was not as vile as Mobutu Sese Seko. Perhaps South African writer Christopher Hope was wrong in claiming that all authoritarians have the same DNA in his seminal book titled *Brothers Under the Skin.* "I would say he was a benevolent leader with a strategy to lead his people. When the West isolates you, they also make sure you are on your own," says Luzamba. Many who advance the argument do not even bother to consider how Ian Smith's Rhodesia overcame international sanctions imposed on it, or the case of a self-sustaining isolated post-Lockerbie Libya under Muamar Gaddafi. The artist's reading of Robert Mugabe also helped put into context what I had observed in the Southern African capitals of Windhoek, Gaborone, Lusaka, and Maputo, which I had been to. In each one of these Pan-African cities, there was at least a road named after Mugabe. Namibia even went the extra mile by naming a clinic after him.

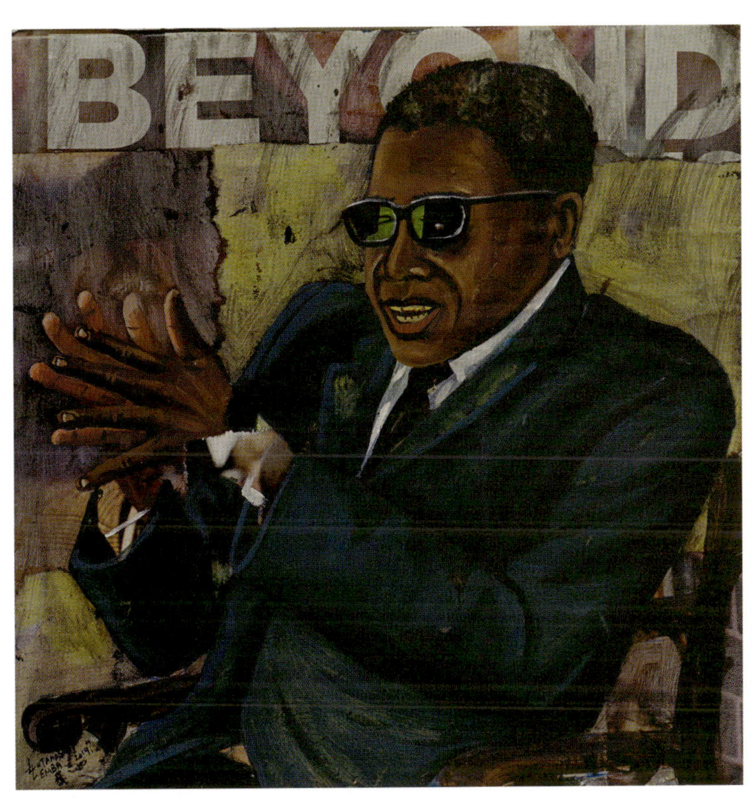

Strategist | Lutanda Zemba Luzamba
2019 | 18cm x18cm | Oil on board

In the work titled *Respect* (2019), Luzamba pays homage to the La Sape movement through a glamorously dressed individual in a white shirt, blue jacket, and hat. The blue monochromatic background lets the viewer engage the central figure without any disturbances. It is a painting that exudes characteristics of elegance and opulence. "The movement of fashionistas has been going on for decades," states Luzamba, and he sees the need to celebrate it in his work. In his practice and what he chooses to portray, I see an artist doing exactly the opposite of what Mutale did with his 'Kaligraphy' drawings. "Let us not undermine our own people by dwelling on the negatives. Let us ignore the pains of the past and embrace the best of the current lifestyle. Even the best of the past," emphasizes Luzamba.

In *Mukubwa T.P.* (2019) and *Learning the Game* (2019), the artist employs the same techniques of collaging newsprints onto a board with the chosen colour combinations making the figures stand out. In the former, he is paying homage to his brother, whom he says is named after his father and therefore sustains the family's legacy. In the latter, the artist is acknowledging politicians who plan strategically and know what moves to make in the same way a chess player makes well-calculated moves as though working through Sun Tzu's "The Art of War".

Luzamba's work has a lot of political statements embedded in it, which may not be so obvious to every viewer. As the artist says, "Sometimes you pick them [the underlying messages] up when you have already fallen in love with the work." He strives to give a chance to the viewer to interpret the work however they like. "Obvious politics keeps certain people away from one's work. Yet everything is politics," says Luzamba.

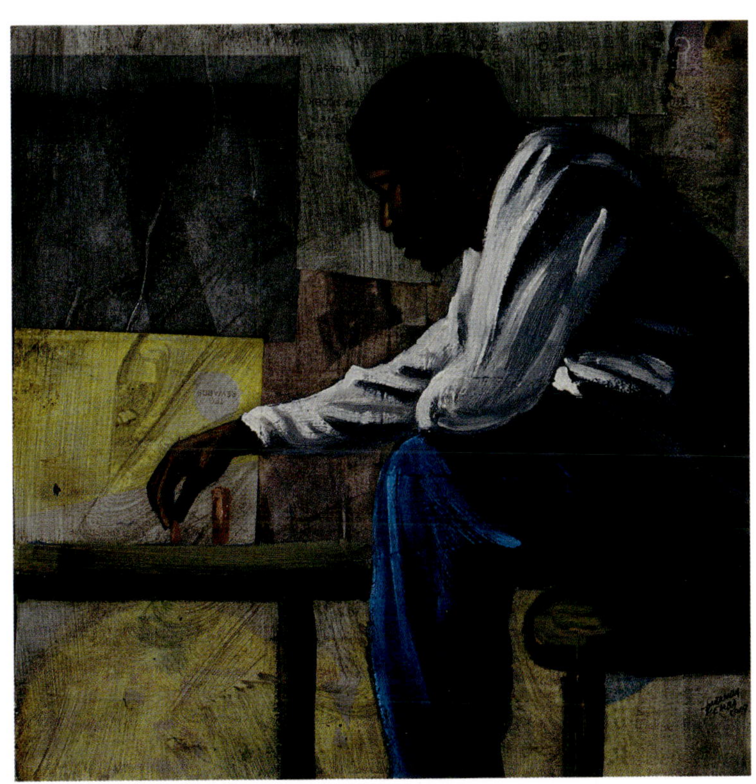

Learning The Game | Lutanda Zemba Luzamba
2019 | 18cm x18cm | Oil on board

PROCESS AND TECHNIQUE

In our conversation, Luzamba is happy to talk about his process. In the pieces with newsprints backgrounds, the artist thoughtfully selects pages from magazines and newspapers, carefully cutting them into the sizes he wants to use. He cautiously selects the newsprint colour combination that he thinks will not distract the final appearance of the main image in place. He glues them onto the canvas and puts a light layer of paint over them and waits for the assemblage to dry. Eventually, he patiently paints the main image over the collage, making sure not to mess the background. Sometimes, the background he creates gives him an idea of what to slot over it. At times, the idea comes first but would be altered by the background. It is a procedure that almost obliterates or collapses parts of the collage. The artist admits that it is a slow and arduous process, but one that he reluctantly revisits when he has the time. For him to master the technique, Luzamba acknowledges the influence of a veteran South African artist named Boyi Molefe, who mentored him in 2002. However, "It is a technique I used more than 20 years ago. I revisited it in 2018 and 2019 and had a show at Ebony Curated. It is a technique I enjoy and still go back to, but it takes time. It draws lots of energy," states Luzamba.

The use of newspapers and newsprints in collage is widespread, even though it is not so popular with the artists from the DRC. It is a practise with a long history dating back to the modernist era when considered in the context of Europe, where artists like Pablo Picasso and Georges Braque applied such found materials in their art. As a medium, the newspapers work well as they are easy to access, and they carry current and past stories, therefore bringing in a bit of history and context. They also address societal issues in interesting ways, albeit most of it comes under sensational headlines. Thus, the newspapers are a vital archive of information. When arranged or juxtaposed carefully in collage, the newsprints can play the role of archives in bringing in the much-needed conceptual relevance that helps the artist formulate the subject, something Luzamba alludes to.

REGIONAL RELEVANCE

Even though Luzamba's work has mainly been looked at from the lens of celebrating the La Sape tradition, its subjects of reference go way beyond that. He comes from a long tradition of Black figurative painting within his country of birth. His oeuvre stretches from the portrayals of the everyday chronicles of his native Congo to the stories of human movement or migration in the region, all presented from a perspective of desiring to see the Black subjects in different Black geographies throughout the world being presented from a position of joy instead of pain. His work carries with it important transnational references with the painter's personality embedded in the narrative as he has lived in the DRC, Zambia, and South Africa, making him a multilingual migratory bird. Luzamba has travelled widely, exhibiting his work in galleries and museums on the continent and beyond.

ARTIST'S BIOGRAPHIES

Rudolf Seibeb was born in 1964 in the city of Okahandja, where he is based and practices from. An autodidact who honed his own craft over the years, Seibeb later enrolled at the John Muafangejo Art Centre in the 1990s, where he met and learned from local art teachers and colleagues. The opportunity enabled the artist to experiment with other media. In 2000, he participated in the SADC Art and Crafts Festival in Windhoek. He took part in three editions of the Triangle Network-sponsored regional workshops (i.e., Tulipamwe International Artists Workshop in Namibia in 2001 and 2003, and the Batapata International Artists Workshop in Harare, Zimbabwe in 2003). The opportunities exposed him to art developments in the region as its participants came from different countries in Southern Africa. The term 'assemblages' describes his layered compositions, which are mostly acrylics on board or canvas, and tend to incorporate found materials the artist collects from his surroundings. Although he mostly depicts the quotidian life of the people around him, Seibeb does not shy away from the topical and controversial socio-political matters in his country. The human face takes centre stage in his colourful depictions. He has participated in several group exhibitions over the years. His first documented solo exhibition titled "Hokverhale – Navigating the Lockdown" appeared at the Project Room in Windhoek in 2020. He won the Commitment Award and the Sculpture Award at the John Muafangejo Art Centre in 2000.

Thebe Phetogo is a multimedia Motswana artist who works with painting, sculpture, and installation. He was born in 1993 in Botswana. Originally trained as a journalist and mostly a self-taught artist, Phetogo later enrolled at the Michaelis School of Fine Art at the University of Cape Town, where he graduated with a Master of Fine Art. His practice engages multiple themes, which include personal identity, gender and sexuality, and heritage and politics. The green screen background has become a hallmark of his paintings in which Black figures painted using shoe polish float on it. Phetogo has done a residency at Art House Foundation in Lagos in 2020, and has also had a solo exhibition at the Kó-Arts Space in Lagos. In 2021, he had a solo show titled "Black Rogues Gallery at Van Amon Co" in Washington DC, as well as "Ko ga Lowe at Guns and Rain" in Johannesburg. His latest solo titled "8 Propositions for the Origin of the Blackbody" took place at Van Amon Co in February 2024. Two of his artworks are included in the "When We See Us: A Century of Black Figuration in Painting" show which was at the Zeitz MOCAA in 2022-2023, and will open at the Kunst museum Basel in Switzerland in May 2024.

(Victor) Mutale Kalinosi Chishimba was born in 1971 in Mungwe in the northern part of Zambia. He attended the local Mungwe primary school. He is a self-taught artist inspired by a childhood friend who attended a school that offered art, and his sister who is a hands-on individual. His first encounter with drawing was in grade 6 in Mr. Chimba's class in Kasama. Mutale attended art classes in grades 8 and 9, completing school in 1991. He wanted to be a soldier because his uncle had died in Zimbabwe's liberation struggle. Years later, he had a burning Pan-Africanist desire to go and fight for the liberation of the Black majority in apartheid South Africa until Nelson Mandela was released. This makes sense when one considers that Mandela's African National Congress had offices in Lusaka. He left Kasama for Livingstone, where he joined the Visual Arts Council in 1995. For four years, he attended national workshops at the Livingstone Museum. He is a multimedia artist who is mainly into drawing, sculpture, and collage.

Nelly Guambe was born in 1987 in Mozambique. She currently lives and works between her home area of Inhambane and Maputo. She holds a Bachelor of Arts in International Relations, attained in 2019 from the University of South Africa in Johannesburg. She developed a keen interest in painting after joining the Mozambican Arts Association, Nucleo de Arte. In her artistic practice, she mostly paints portraits of women she knows and those encountered on the streets of Maputo. Their faces and gazes are quite telling, as they leave viewers with a lot of unanswered questions. In 2019, Nelly won the inaugural Africa First-sponsored Emerging Painting Invitational prize in Harare. She also won the Mozal prize in the category of 'Artes Plasticas' in Mozambique in the same year. She co-founded the Deal Creative Space in Maputo. Her work featured in a group show at Stevenson Gallery in 2018, and this was followed by a solo show titled "CARAS" at the same gallery. She has taken part in the Investec Cape Town Art Fair with Guns and Rain Gallery; had a solo exhibition, "Olhares", at the Portuguese Cultural Institute in Maputo. In 2018, she featured at the 1:54 Contemporary African Art Fair with the London-based Ed Cross Fine Art. She also featured in the About Face group exhibition at Stevenson Gallery in Cape Town in 2018.

Lutanda Zemba Luzamba was born in 1973 in the Democratic Republic of Congo. He lives and works in Cape Town, South Africa. He attended the Evelyn Hone College of Applied Arts and Commerce in Lusaka, Zambia. In his practice, Luzamba mostly depicts African men elegantly dressed in Western-style suits in the La Sape fashion, a tradition which rose to prominence in both Congo-Kinshasa and Congo-Brazzaville. In the former, the traditions had resistance undertones to it as the country's leader, Mobuto Sese Seko, had banned the suits in the 1960s. Luzamba is a Pan-Africanist who portrays the migration narratives of Africans with dignity and celebrates the achievements of some of Africa's visionary leaders. Yet, his personal journey is always embedded in the transnational stories he portrays, himself having lived and worked in different countries. He previously participated in the Africa South Arts Initiative (ASAI) workshops in Cape Town. He has had several solo shows in different countries including recent ones like "Totem" at Ebony Curated in 2023, and "Kitendi" at Galarie Studer in Abidjan, Cote D'Ivoire in 2023. His work is also included in the "When We See Us: A Century of Black Figuration in Paintin"g show, which was at the Zeitz MOCAA in 2022-2023, and is scheduled to open at the Kunstmuseum Basel in Switzerland in May 2024.

AUTHOR'S BIOGRAPHY

Barnabas Ticha Muvhuti is an art historian and writer with research interests in the modern and contemporary art practices of Southern Africa. He holds a PhD in Art History from Rhodes University in South Africa. A member of the RIT research project of The Fletcher School at Tufts University (USA), he writes extensively on the integration experiences of migrants in Southern Africa. He has worked as a gallery assistant at the AVA Gallery in Cape Town and the Centre for African Studies Gallery (UCT), a research assistant and project manager at the Centre for Curating the Archive (UCT), and a research assistant for the Curatorial Department at the Zeitz MOCAA Museum (helping research for the ground-breaking When We See Us exhibition). He has written several exhibition reviews, opinion pieces, and carried out multiple interviews/conversations with artists and curators. He contributed to the African Artists: From 1882 to Now and ARTTHROB_: 25 Years of Art Writing in South Africa publications. Ticha was the first recipient of the ARAK Collection Art Writing Residency Fellowship, May-November 2023.

CONTRIBUTOR'S BIOGRAPHY

Dr. Andrew Mulenga, a leading authority on art history in Zambia, has been recognized for his contributions to the country's artistic community. He was awarded the 2012 CNN African Journalist of the Year for Arts & Culture and a Media Institute of Southern Africa (MISA) award in 2015 for his work in arts journalism while pursuing an MA in Art History at Rhodes University in South Africa. He has been awarded scholarships for his MA and PhD in art history by the National Research Foundation of South Africa and the Andrew Mellon Foundation in the United States.

Mulenga has given public talks and seminars for upcoming art writers in Zambia, as well as lectures on Zambian visual art at several international universities. He has also served as an art history lecturer at the Zambian Open University in Lusaka and has been the resident art critic at The Post Newspapers and published a weekly art column called "Andrew Mulenga's Hole in the Wall" for almost 15 years.

Currently, he plans to gather various articles into a published anthology, highlighting the importance of documentation in the visual arts industry and the insightful look into one ofthe most important periods in Zambian art history. He is also the deputy vice chancellor of Open Window University for the Creative Arts in Lusaka, Zambia, which offers undergraduate and postgraduate degrees in creative arts fields such as photography, film-making, graphic design, and creative writing.

BIBLIOGRAPHY

Books

Hassan, Salah M., and Olu Oguibe. Authentic/Ex-Centric: Conceptualism in Contemporary African Art. Ithaca, NY: Forum for African Arts, 2001.

Morley, Simon. The Simple Truth: The Monochrome in Modern Art. London: Reaktion Books, 2020.

Okeke-Agulu, Chika, Joseph L. Underwood, and Chika Okeke-Agulu, eds. African Artists: From 1882 to Now. London: Phaidon Press, 2021.

Kreamer, Christine Mullen, Mary Nooter Roberts, Elizabeth Harney, and Allyson Purpura. Inscribing Meaning: Writing and Graphic Systems in African Art. Washington, DC: Smithsonian National Museum of African Art, 2007.

Journal Articles

Kerkham, Ruth. "Konse Kubili: Kalinosi Mutale and Anawana Haloba." Nka: Journal of Contemporary African Art, no. 21 (Fall 2007): 124–25.

Theses and Dissertations

Moolman, Tiani. "Environmental Reasoning of Secondary-Level Schoolchildren: Case Study of Okahandja, Namibia." PhD diss., Stellenbosch University, 2015.

Mulenga, Andrew Mukuka. "Contemporary Zambian Art, Conceptualism and the 'Global' Art World." Master's thesis, Rhodes University, 2016.

Phetogo, Thebe. "Bogasatswana: Rebuilding the Boat While Sailing." Master's thesis, University of Cape Town, 2019.

Exhibition Catalogues and Texts

Mawhayi, Khanyisile. "Totem." In Ebony Curated, 2023.

Proud, Hayden. "Bridges to the Present: Zimbabwean Painting at the Crossroads." In Five Bhobh: Painting at the End of an Era, edited by Sven Christian and Tandazani Dhlakama, 88–104. Cape Town: Zeitz MOCAA, 2018.

Rogge, Jo. "Unmourned Bodies." AVA Gallery, Cape Town, March 9–April 20, 2023.

Websites and Online Sources

Al Jazeera English. "Anatomy of a Bribe." YouTube video, 2020. https://www.youtube.com/watch?app=desktop&v=_FJ1TB0nwHs

Al Jazeera English. “Gold Mafia-The Laundry Service.” YouTube video, 2023. https://www.youtube.com/watch?v=evWEuVR1XIs&t=106s

Challis, Sam. "Rock Art: How South Africa’s Coat of Arms Got to Feature an Ancient San Painting." The Conversation, December 20, 2022. https://theconversation.com/rock-art-how-south-africas-coat-of-arms-got-to-feature-an-ancient-san-painting-195297

Chigumadzi, Panashe. "Sankofa and the Afterlives of Makerere." Los Angeles Review of Books, June 1, 2021. https://lareviewofbooks.org/article/sankofa-and-the-afterlives-of-makerere/

"Frontline States." South African History Online. Accessed December 25, 2023. https://www.sahistory.org.za/article/frontline-states

Gabbai, Arik. "What Makes Humans Different? Fiction and Cooperation: Historian Yuval Noah Harari Previews His Book on the Past and Future of Homo Sapiens." Smithsonian Magazine, May 2015. https://www.smithsonianmag.com/arts-culture/what-makes-humans-different-fiction-and-cooperation-180953986/#:~:text=All%20other%20animals%20use%20their,world%20and%20this%20is%20money

Jamal, Ashraf. "The ARAK Collection." MOL 42, Art Times (South Africa).
Krempel, Ulrich. "El Loko." Artco Gallery. Accessed December 25, 2023. https://www.artco-gallery.com/artists/43-el-loko/overview/

"The Fishrot Scandal." Platform to Protect Whistleblowers in Africa. Accessed December 25, 2023. https://www.pplaaf.org/cases/fishrot.html#

Other Sources

Ellenberger, Vivian. "History and Prehistory of Botswana." Botswana Notes and Records 4 (1972): 135–36.

Guns & Rain. Thebe Phetogo – Ko ga Lowe. 2021.

Muvhuti, Barnabas Ticha. Personal communication during field trip, Lusaka, Zambia, 2023.

Introduction
Andrew Mulenga

Author
Barnabas Ticha Muvhuti

Design
Mussavir Sheikh

Collection Coordinator
Thasni Pattathil

Photography
Maaz Mansoor

Logistic
MD Arshad Khan

Publisher
Hamad Bin Khalifa University Press